DR. JERRY BACK

CAN WE TALK?
...ABOUT MATTERS OF THIS LIFE

WINEPRESS WP PUBLISHING

ISBN 1-57921-247-6
Library of Congress Catalog Card Number: 99-65340

CONTENTS

Part III:
A Better Way

"Why?"
This nagging question screamed from the front page of *U.S. News & World Report*. The editors continued, "After a murderous rampage in Colorado, America confronts the alienation that grips so many teenagers."[1] The occasion was the shooting and bombing at Columbine High School in Littleton, Colorado, that took place April 20, 1999.

One positive result of the tragic event is that there is a consensus across the land that something is radically wrong with the American dream and that ignoring it will not make it go away. A reoccurring statement heard in the halls of Congress and the halls of public and private schools alike is "It can happen here" followed by the question "Are we ready for it?" Almost everyone expects it to happen again and again with increasing frequency and violence.

At the center of this human tragedy, whether he wanted to be or not, was Brian Warner, AKA "Marilyn

Manson." This purveyor of hate and evil and his band have been one of the links connecting a series of school shootings because nearly all of the shooters have been avid fans of his form of entertainment. His sponsors decided to cancel the last five concerts of his U.S. tour as a result of the massacre. According to one news report, "Manson said he is bowing out of the five shows out of respect for the Littleton victims. 'It's not a great atmosphere to be out playing rock 'n' roll shows—for us or the fans,' he said, adding that he blames ignorance, hatred and access to guns for the tragedy."[2] Others who ran for cover were members of the National Rifle Association, who curtailed their national convention that was to be held in Denver the week following the shooting.

There was much finger pointing taking place with many talking heads giving "expert opinions." The news wires sizzled. Talks shows were inundated. Many expressed their own opinions as to what had gone wrong. One important question begging an answer is "Do we really want to know?" Like so many times in the face of human tragedy, many people are satisfied with an answer that suits them, lets them off the hook, or provides a soothing balm without the radical surgery that might be necessary to truly rid society of the cancerous growth metastasizing throughout the country. Too often we are like the man confronted by Jesus at the pool at Bethesda. He laid by the pool for thirty-eight years waiting for someone to put him into the water. Jesus asked him, "Do you wish to get well?" (John 5:6).

At first, this seems like a cruel question. Had not this man demonstrated his desire to get well by his persistence all those years? Yet anytime there is a protracted illness this question is legitimate. Because of the way our minds work, we are capable of saying we want a solution to the illness while all the time not really wanting to be cured, because we fear the cure or the changes we must make more than the illness itself.

As you read this book, you may be a parent who is asking, "Why?" Perhaps you are seeking answers as to how you can help your children avoid some of the pitfalls facing young people growing up in today's culture. You may be a pastor or youth worker seeking how you can help the youth who are coming to you for guidance. It is my earnest prayer that some young people will have the courage and tenacity to read this book and to interact with the concepts presented in it.

Perhaps you are a young person going through your own personal struggles. In this book, I will share with you some of the problems I faced growing up. I praise God that I was not faced with some of the situations you are facing today: drugs, violence in entertainment, and free sex along with the risks associated with it. Still, whoever you are and whatever you are facing, there is hope. Your struggles may not be identical to mine, but there is still hope no matter what those problems are. This hope is not found in the pages of this book. This book is simply a guide to lead you to the only person who can help you, Jesus Christ. May your journey lead you to Him.

When seeking to provide an answer to today's problems, one difficulty is that we are a society conditioned to hear sixty-second sound bites. Yet the problems are so complex that no sixty-second sound bite can answer them. Some of the material in this book cannot be couched in such a format. It has taken years for me to even begin to understand the truths I will attempt to explain. You may want to skip some of the details and read them later after you see the main idea of what I am saying. It is my earnest prayer that you will take the time to understand what is presented here and that it will help you understand more clearly your answers to the questions raised in this book.

As a result of the shooting and bombing at Columbine High, two incidents in my life lead me to believe that perhaps I can give at least a partial answer to the question "Why?" The first was a conversation over dinner my wife and I had with friends. It was years since we had been together with this couple, and we had much catching up to do. Yet world events, particularly the Littleton massacre, dominated our conversation. At one point, my wife said, "It gives me comfort to know that God is in control."

The immediate response was, "That's just a platitude."

I knew what she meant by her comment and, at first, thought of defending her. Yet I also sensed what our friend meant by his remark. My wife was speaking from a strong belief in the goodness and sovereignty of God. Our friend, on the other hand, was speaking from the point of view that the infection permeating every fabric of society is so pervasive that no trite answer will do. He would not settle for an easy answer, nor would he accept a "We have all the answers" attitude.

This is not the time for Christians to stand up and say, "We have all the answers." Even the most elementary view of church history dispels that notion. More wars have been fought in the name of religion than for any other reason. The Christian religion is no exception. Most of the conflicts presently raging around the world are fired by hatred and bigotry rooted in religion. Marilyn Manson does not have a corner on such vile human emotions.

If those of us who identify ourselves as Christians hope to have any part in the dialogue, we must come down off our self-constructed pedestals and acknowledge that we do not always practice what we preach. Perhaps much of what we preach is a poor representation of the religion we profess. By *religion*, I mean that which we do as an expression of our faith. The term is used in this way in the Book of James, where we read:

> If anyone thinks himself to be religious, and yet does not bridle his tongue but deceives his [own] heart, this man's religion is worthless. Pure and undefiled religion in the sight of [our] God and Father is this: to visit orphans and widows in their distress, [and] to keep oneself unstained by the world. (James 1:26–27)

As a parent, a Christian in ministry, or a young person, the very reason you are reading this book indicates that you are concerned about matters of this life and are seeking ways to avoid tragedies like the one that took place in Littleton. Following the shooting, the cameras focused on some of the victims who had a strong faith in Jesus Christ. It was encouraging to hear about them. Yet there are many young people today who either have rejected Christianity or are having difficulty putting their faith into practice. Why does the Christian faith seem to work for some and not for others? How can you make it work for yourself and your family? I, too, have had difficulty putting my faith into practice. I wish that someone had been able to sit down with me early in my Christian experience and explain the philosophies and principles discussed in this book.

Christians as a whole are experiencing as much conflict and alienation as any other group in society. Our track record in the area of family values, such as abortion, adultery, pornography, and other forms of antisocial and addictive behavior, are not much better than those who do not claim to be Christians. If we do know the answer—and I sincerely believe we do—there must be a problem with the way we, the Christian community as a whole, are applying what we claim to know. This failure compels us to ask the same question, Why? No platitudes will suffice. The events unfolding around the world demand that we not simply give an answer but live the answer we give.

This brings me to the second event that convinced me that I needed to formulate my own answer to this question. My son, David, called me long distance to express his reaction to the massacre and subsequent media dialogue. David is now twenty-three years old. When He was in middle school we lived in Littleton, Colorado, near where the shooting occurred. This added a special poignancy to what took place at Columbine High. However, it was not the massacre itself that prompted his phone call.

David was watching a CNN program in which a psychologist was explaining the telltale signs indicating a child was about to go over the edge. One of the first signs, he said, was anger. My son's reaction was, "Dad, I was there!" By this, he meant that he had been angry himself.

When we lived in Colorado, I was the director of a Christian organization. It was a particularly stressful time for our family. I knew that David was not handling the stress well, but I was not able to help him because of my own situation. As a family, we did make it through that difficult period in our lives and now realize how close we all came to going over the edge.

As we reminisced on the phone, I reminded David that when I was the same age as he was in Littleton I had a violent temper. At a very young age, my biological family disintegrated. Subsequently, I became a ward of the state and entered the foster-care system. Being passed from family to family, I experienced many different types of discipline. In the late 1940s, methods of discipline were often cruel. Much of what was then called discipline has since been outlawed as child abuse.

At the age of eight I was adopted. My adopting parents had already experienced many personal and marital problems before I was adopted. Those problems spilled over to me afterward. There were episodes of anger that resulted in violent fights exacerbated by the abuse of alcohol. This made the normal struggles of adopting a child even more difficult to overcome. As the years passed, parental discipline turned into beatings. The instrument used in these beatings was anything close at hand: a pitchfork, a barn shovel, rolled up haywire. I soon learned to anticipate when the anger would turn violent and, out of sheer defense, learned to get angrier faster than my father did.

Part of my frustration as a child was that my adopted father was a well-known and respected member of society. During my early teenage years, he was a leader in several fraternal organizations, chairman of the board of the school district where I attended school, chairman of the board of county commissioners, and dairy products commissioner for the state. This led me to conclude that most of the anger and violence in our home was my fault, and I was sure everyone else thought so too.

As I look back on those years, I can appreciate the inner turmoil that countless teenagers experience today. Three times I ran away from home. Three times I was locked in solitary confinement in the county jail by orders from my father. Finally, during one violent encounter, I was struck from behind with a barn shovel and then repeatedly stabbed with a pitchfork. The only thing that saved my life was the heavy coat I was wearing.

After a day lying dazed in the basement of the family home without any treatment for my head wound, my father drove me to the county jail on his way to the Elks Club. As the jailer was booking me, he noticed my head wound and rushed me to the hospital emergency room, where I was treated for two gashes in my scalp. That time I refused to go back home and insisted that I be allowed to appear before the juvenile judge, the only man in the county I felt I could trust.

On the day of the hearing, the county prosecuting attorney accompanied my father and mother into the courtroom. I was alone to face my parents as my accusers. However, after a few questions by the judge, the prosecutor told my father, "I can't help you," and walked out. As a result of that hearing, I was made ward of the court and was under the court's protection until I graduated from high school. My high-school graduation was held on a Friday night. My father did not attend. On Monday morning, I was inducted into the Navy, the only way I felt I could escape my situation.

By the time I graduated from high school, I had a well-developed violent temper and was searching for a way to overcome it. In the Navy, I met some individuals who served with a Christian organization called The Navigators. They introduced me to a man who lived a long time ago, Jesus of Nazareth. I accepted Him as my savior, but my life did not immediately change. I still had many of the bad habits I had learned back on the farm: drinking, smoking, swearing, and outbursts of anger. The anger was so ingrained in me that I often had nightmares that I would one day lose my temper and kill someone.

The task of putting my life together was not accomplished overnight, nor was it simply a decision on my part. It was a learning process. I had to learn to see things from a totally different point of view, from God's point of view. It is this change in thinking that this book is all about. The process taking place in me is not complete, nor will it be this side of eternity. Sometimes, I have not been able to see the progress in my life, but others have.

When my daughter, Tamara, was in high school, she and I loved to take each other out to dinner. She is now married with two children and a growing career. Our times together over dinner are now few and far between. The last time she took me out to dinner, we discussed our faith in Christ. She said something to me that I will always cherish. She said she believes that her faith in Christ is genuine because she has seen the change that faith has produced in me.

The title of this book, *Can We Talk?* is based on the apostle Paul's assumption that Christians should be able to explain some of the underlying causes of problems in this life. In 1 Corinthians 6:3–4, Paul warns Christians against taking each other to court. The phrase "matters of this life" is translated from one Greek word, *biotikos*. It refers to the affairs of this present life in contrast to our eternal existence with God. While this word is used in only one other context in the New Testament, it is a very important concept. The practical application of what Paul instructed is that if anyone should be able to give an answer regarding the problems in society, it should be Christians.

In this book, I want to explain the journey I have traveled thus far and how the changes in my life have come about. These changes do not come from simple platitudes, nor are they always instantaneous, although they can be for some. The journey begins with what the Bible calls being born again, born from above (John 3:3), or born of God (John 1:12–13). My heartfelt prayer is that this book will help someone who is struggling with matters of this life find help in overcoming those difficulties.

PART I

THE IMPORTANCE OF RELATIONSHIPS
AND COMMUNICATION TO
MATTERS OF THIS LIFE

CHAPTER ONE

Healthy Relationships: The Key to Fulfillment

Fulfillment in life comes when we build healthy relationships. God never intended for us to face life alone. In the beginning, Adam was created first to have a relationship with God and then to have a relationship with Eve. In the Garden of Eden the first effect of sin was to separate Adam and Eve from God and then to destroy the relationships within the first family. The God-ordained relationship of marriage and family was impacted by sin with devastating results. Some may discount the Bible's teaching regarding creation and the Fall, but no one can discount the fact that relationships are in serious trouble in America today. The dysfunctional family is undeniable proof that sin entered the human race; and the consequences of sin were passed on to all of us.

Recently, while waiting in a doctor's office, a little eighteen-month-old girl came toddling up to me with a smile and held out some stickers for me to see. Her mother came chasing after her. The mother was a beautiful young girl who could not have been more than sixteen years of age. I fought back tears as I thought of the struggles those two young girls were going to experience in life—a mother and a daughter not more than fourteen years apart. How will they ever survive in a world that believes that healthy relationships are not necessary and may not be possible? Who is the father of the child? How is he coping with his responsibilities? Is he able to meet those responsibilities? Does he even care?

The evidence of dysfunctional relationships is everywhere. When I counsel young couples in premarital counseling, I notice a pattern. Whether they come from broken, dysfunctional homes, or stable homes, there is fear and uncertainty. They often doubt their ability to form enduring, healthy relationships. Some do not trust themselves. Some do not trust the partner they plan to marry. How can they possibly achieve what so few are able to achieve today: a happy, healthy home? The situation is vastly more complicated if they have already engaged in premarital sex, if children have been conceived out of wedlock, or if they have already experienced a failed marriage.

The message that God wants each of us to hear is that it is possible to establish and maintain healthy relationships today in spite of sin and in spite of the cynicism of a world full of dysfunctional relationships. Healthy relationships do not happen simply because we are born into this world. Even when families do not fall apart, building healthy relationships is still difficult.

Regardless of our experiences in the past, we can build healthy relationships. If we have already violated the sacred bond of matrimony by engaging in practices that God declares to be sins against Him, against others, and against ourselves, this too can be overcome.

The Psalmist wrote, "If Thou, LORD, shouldst mark iniquities, O Lord, who could stand? But there is forgiveness with Thee, that Thou mayest be feared. I wait for the LORD, my soul does wait, and in His word do I hope" (Psalm 130:3–5). It would be better if we could build relationships without the millstones of sin and guilt around our neck. For most of us, that is not an option, because we already have this millstone necklace. Still, regardless of our sin and guilt, we can come to God and He will show us the way to build healthy relationships.

HINDRANCES TO BUILDING RELATIONSHIPS

It seems as if the world has discovered the importance of relationships. When we have a little money in our pocket, or something else someone wants, the whole world tries to convince us we are related to them. The advertising industry exploits relationships in order to sell their products. Politicians try to convince us that they are somehow related to us to get our vote. Even churches promote relationships to attract new members. We need to be careful. Many times, the high-pressure sales pitch that touts relationships is really *manipulation*, rather than a sincere offer of goods and services. How many times do we fall for the sales pitch only to find that the product is defective and that when we need service the huckster who sold us the goods is already out of town?

Manipulation Hinders Relationships

Simply because we have something someone else wants does not mean that they have a relationship with us or that we have any responsibility to them. A good example is the telephone solicitor. He has a habit of calling and interfering with relationships that far exceed him in importance. People involved in television, radio, the Internet, and the ubiquitous telephone all tout themselves as bridges to help us build relationships. We are told that we can interact with the world through these mediums and build relationships all over the world. Supposedly, it is part of the global mentality so popular today.

Because my ministry is in the area of counseling and conflict management, I frequently receive e-mail from individuals seeking counsel in how to deal with conflict in their lives. One individual contacted me to explain that her church and pastor were involved in a conflict. Over several weeks, I continued to receive messages from her with questions that I tried to answer. Gradually, however, I began to suspect that this person was not who she claimed to be. In the first few e-mails, she presented herself as an uneducated person who was simply concerned for her pastor and church. As the e-mails became more and more personal, I began to suspect that she was not as uneducated as she had claimed.

I insisted that, to continue the relationship, I would need to know that her husband was aware of our correspondence and that he approved.

Finally, I was asked to reveal some personal information that I did not feel she needed to know. As a hook, she revealed personal information to me about herself that may or may not have been true. I had no way of knowing. When I refused to disclose the information she requested and did not respond as quickly as she expected, she became angry with me and sent a very terse message. In reply, I explained that I had God-given responsibilities to fulfill in biblical relationships. I did not consider a relationship over the Internet important enough to supersede any of these relationships, and, in fact, it was a very low priority. I went on to encourage her to reconsider her biblical relationships and her responsibilities in them. It was my intention to maintain a proper balance, and I encouraged her to do the same.

I did not hear from her for some weeks. Finally, when I did, she dropped any pretense of being uneducated or in need of counsel. While I do not know to this day what her motives were, it is obvious that she was using me to achieve some personal gain. It may have merely been the process of building an Internet network. It may have been curiosity. It may have been far more sinister. Whatever her reason, I have not replied to her, nor do I intend to until I am sure of the purpose and scope of that relationship and what my responsibilities before God are in it.

A relationship is not simply an easy tool to get something out of someone. If the relationship is genuine, all parties in the relationship will benefit from it. There is a lot of discussion about ways to motivate people. Often, the last thing mentioned—if it is mentioned at all—is the on-going relationship between the motivator and the one being motivated. Motivation without a relationship is manipulation. As we will see later on, a healthy relationship is one in which everyone in the relationship is willing to accept responsibility for the relationship with the expectation of sharing personally from that relationship.

Understanding the relationship between the motivator and the motivated is doubly true for young people today who lack the discernment to know whether or not the one who is claiming to have a relationship with them is exploiting them. It seems like an acceptable part of life today to say and do anything in order to take advantage of others. Children need to be taught early in life to recognize the difference between relationship, manipulation, and exploitation. Many never learn and suffer great harm in life. The greatest harm is the loss of trust in others that comes when an individual becomes aware that he or she has been exploited.

Self-Centeredness Hinders Relationships

We often hear people talk of having a relationship with self. In this book, what is meant by *relationship* is the interaction between two or more people. In some contexts it might be correct to speak of having a relationship with self, but most of the time this is a misnomer. An overemphasis upon self—self-awareness, self-esteem, and self-concept—leads to a worship of self often referred to as *meism*. Meism is the product of a false philosophy or worldview. It may be an attempt to see ourselves as central to every issue, as if we are the center of the universe and everything that happens in the world affects us, depends upon us, or benefits us. This self-centeredness is at the core of many problems in society.

The nightly newscast fosters the attitude of meism. Newscasters tell us that we must stay tuned so that we can see and hear in living color and surround-sound the latest earth-shaking event. When there is not enough hard news, they create news to fill up the time. This adds to the difficulty of discerning what is important and what is not. What is particularly disturbing is to hear them say, "You will only hear this late-breaking exclusive news coverage on our station." In this way, they portray us as the center of the universe. And they are right there with us making sure that we interpret the universe from their point of view.

This book is about building relationships with other people. We will see that our thought life and self-concept have a bearing upon our ability to build healthy relationships. We will discover that, if we constantly see ourselves at the center of every event in life, then our self-concept will be warped. This will have a definite negative impact upon our relationships with others. The ideal would be to be completely selfless. This is not possible in this life, but it is a goal toward which we must all strive if we are to learn how to build healthy relationships.

THREE LEVELS OF RELATIONSHIPS

We are members of the human race and live in a community of human beings. If we are going to survive, we need to understand the nature of relationships, how to build healthy relationships, and what our responsibilities are in those relationships. Some relationships we enter into because of circumstances, and others by choice. Technology has made it possible to bridge the gap of time and space and to reach around the world. Technology can be a valuable tool for building healthy relationships, or it can destroy relationships. Therefore, we need to understand relationships in general, and then we need to enter into relationships with due care.

The starting point in building healthy relationships is to recognize that there are three levels. The first level is relationships of *circumstance*: We just happen to be in the same place at the same time. These relationships arise without our making a definite decision to enter into them. The second level is relationships of *purpose*: We have something in common with someone else and seek to accomplish some goal in partnership with him or her. These we enter into by choice. The third level is relationships of *fulfillment*: We become partners moving in a positive direction together to accomplish the will of God. These are relationships in which we have learned to work through difficulties and conflicts to the point of success.

The commonality in each of these levels is that we have God-given responsibilities in every relationship.

Level 1: Relationships of Circumstance

A relationship of circumstance might be a crowd of individuals at a movie theater. We have responsibilities even in such impersonal situations. For example, we owe it to each other to be courteous and considerate. How many times have you been in a public gathering with people who spoiled it for everyone else because of their rudeness? This demonstrates a lack of courtesy and consideration for others, which is common among many in society. Such behavior makes it more difficult to feel comfortable in a crowd.

The importance of relationships of circumstance can be seen when we drive our cars seventy miles an hour down the highway. A lack of courtesy and consideration on the part of just one driver can be deadly to others on the highway. Society cannot function without basic relational skills and the acceptance of personal responsibilities in relationships of circumstance. Yet it has become sport among many today to be as discourteous and thoughtless toward others as possible. They think it is funny. If the trend continues, society will be destroyed.

I grew up believing that each member of society has a responsibility to other members of society to stay on the correct side of the road while driving and to respect the rights and personal property of others as well as public property. I once believed that if I looked out for the other guy, he would look out for me. This has all been turned upside down by a culture that disdains such simple truth and laughs at anyone dumb enough to believe it. This mocking attitude is reinforced constantly through the media and at all levels of society. The media condemns those who "draw within the lines" as narrow and dull. We will look at some philosophies fueling this attitude in other chapters.

Relationships of circumstance are relationships we did not choose to enter into. We might wrongly assume that, since we did not choose them, we should not be held accountable for them. However, God has defined our responsibilities in every possible relationship, whether we chose those relationships or not.

One relationship of circumstance is the relationship of a child to a parent. We are not given a choice of parents. Yet God has made it very clear that how we relate to our parents is very important to Him and to us. In the Ten Commandments, God commanded, "Honor your father and your mother, that your days may be prolonged in the land which the LORD your God gives you" (Exodus 20:12). Paul reminded the church of this command. He wrote, "HONOR YOUR FATHER AND MOTHER (which is the first commandment with a promise)" (Ephesians 6:2). Even though we do not choose our parents, God still holds us accountable for the way we treat our parents. In fact, how we treat our parents will have a profound effect on the course our lives will take.

Another important relationship of circumstance is that of a brother or sister. We do not have the privilege of choosing them, but we still have a responsibility to build healthy relationships with them. God does not place on us the responsibility of honoring them in the same way He does honoring our parents.

In God's plan, a relationship with a brother or sister is not as important as the relationship to a parent. A healthy relationship with a sibling can be very beneficial. However, the need to get along and work through conflicts does not hold the same urgency as it does with parents. Time, distance, and circumstances may weaken the impact a relationship with siblings has in our lives. This is not true with regard to parents.

Even after we leave home to start a family of our own, our parents play a significant role in our family as role models for our children. Because of the breakdown of the family in America and because of mobility, the important role grandparents play in families has been overlooked. Also often overlooked is the impact the behavior of a child has upon a parent well into adulthood. When we choose a marriage partner, in effect, we are choosing another family member to whom our parents will need to relate. That is why in the Old Testament and even in the New Testament, parents played a significant role in who their children married. We do not have such conventionalities today, and the choice of a marriage partner is often made even against the wishes and counsel of parents. When that happens, parents are faced with relationships of circumstance and the problems that arise from them.

This first level of relationships, relationships of circumstance, can be as binding upon us as any relationship in which we had a choice at the beginning. We need the guidance of God's Word to teach us what our responsibilities are in these relationships, and we need the power of God to meet these responsibilities.

Through the years, I have had the privilege of working temporary jobs through temporary employment agencies. I came to view these experiences as opportunities to build relationships of circumstance. Those of us in full-time ministry often find ourselves far from the real world because our ministry confines us to working with Christians in Christian organizations with Christian goals. On the other hand, working in temporary job situations can often thrust us into unplanned situations.

When preparing to go out on a temporary assignment, I prayed that God would show me His divine appointment. Each time I took a temporary job, I believed God had a plan for me to rub shoulders with someone whom I might never have met otherwise. This provided opportunities to witness to others through my relationship with them and to demonstrate the love of God to them. Through this type of work, I met a number of individuals who, by the end of my assignment, confided—some with tears—that they were my divine appointment.

John wrote about a trip that Jesus made to Galilee with His disciples. Concerning this trip we read:

> When therefore the Lord knew that the Pharisees had heard that Jesus was making and baptizing more disciples than John (although Jesus Himself was not baptizing, but His disciples were), He left Judea and

departed again into Galilee. And *He had to* pass through Samaria. (John 4:1–4, italics mine)

The Greek term translated "He had to" is an important term. The term first means "to bind."[1] In some passages it has the idea of arresting and then binding as one in authority might bind a prisoner. Therefore, John tells us that Jesus was bound by divine authority to go through Samaria. The circumstances that led to this were because of the threat against Jesus that was beginning to develop in Judea, which made staying there dangerous.

We are not told why Jesus chose the shorter route through Samaria to Galilee, rather than going around Samaria by crossing the Jordan River, which was Jewish tradition. However, the fact that He stayed in the village two days suggests that haste was not the reason.

He had to take the route through Samaria so He could meet and could engage in conversation the woman at the well and could lead the Samaritans to trust in Him. This fact underscores the reason why John included this event at this place in his Gospel. John wanted to show that, while the Jews in Judea rejected Him, the Samaritans, who were hated by the Jews, received Him. They were His divine appointment.

Armed with this concept, we need to view relationships of circumstance as divine appointments. These may be opportunities to share Christ and to build relationships through which we can demonstrate the Christian life to a lost world. This is true lifestyle evangelism and is far more effective than any canned approach to sharing the gospel. Many times, it is an opportunity to encourage brothers and sisters in Christ in the marketplace in ways that can never be demonstrated at church on Sunday morning.

Looking back over my life with this concept of relationships of circumstance in mind, I can see how the hand of God was working in my life long before I ever understood who God is or how one enters into His family. There are many painful memories that could be roots of bitterness. However, looking back with this perspective causes the poison of bitterness and anger to drain away from the personal injuries sustained at the hand of others long ago. Like Joseph to his brothers, I can say to those who have inflicted pain upon me, "And as for you, you meant evil against me, [but] God meant it for good . . ." (Genesis 50:20). For the believer, every relationship is an opportunity—a divine appointment—for good as we live out His plan for our lives. This truth brings much healing to my life.

Level 2: Relationships of Purpose

In the second level, relationships of purpose, we find ourselves in situations where we expect something beyond simple courtesy and consideration from each other. We enter into these relationships by choice and assume the responsibility for our part in the relationships. These relationships can be as simple as opening a bank account, acquiring a credit card, or buying a home in a particular neighborhood. Or they could be as complex as choosing a marriage partner, a business partner, or a church family.

Each of these is a relationship of purpose because we choose to enter the relationships. Often there are other individuals who choose to enter into the relationship also. The bank chooses to provide services for a price. The credit card company and mortgage lender choose to loan money with the expectation that the money will be paid back with interest. Each relationship of purpose should be viewed from the standpoint of mutual benefit and shared responsibilities. It is important to realize that what to us is a relationship of purpose because we choose to enter into it, to another person may be a relationship of circumstance because they do not have a choice. The relationship is forced upon them through no action on their part.

One very important relationship of purpose is the sexual relationship. In God's plan, the sexual relationship was given to provide enjoyment for those involved in it. But physical pleasure is not the only purpose. In fact, when we seriously consider its purpose from the point of view of the Bible, the responsibilities of each partner are astronomical when compared to the single purpose of pleasure.

That fact is lost in the raging debate over abortion. One side claims the right to define sex as simply for pleasure while the other defends the rights of the unborn child. This issue will never be settled until the personal responsibilities of each individual are clearly understood and accepted.

Accepting responsibility means giving up something for the good of the other person(s) in the relationship. While this is true in every relationship, it is doubly true in the sexual relationship. Failure to identify, accept, and fulfill one's God-given responsibilities means the failure of that relationship. Even when our behavior in any given relationship is considered legal and acceptable by society, if it violates God's moral standard, the relationship cannot succeed. In fact, the Bible makes it clear that God will hold us accountable for our failure to fulfill the responsibilities He established for us.

Solomon wrote to his son and reminded him:

> Rejoice, young man, during your childhood, and let your heart be pleasant during the days of young manhood. And follow the impulses of your heart and the desires of your eyes. Yet know that God will bring you to judgment for all these things. (Ecclesiastes 11:9)

Perhaps the most significant relationship of purpose is that of a parent to a child. God has given adults the ability to choose when children will be born. Along with this choice comes the responsibility of caring for the child. To the child, it is a relationship of circumstance. To the parents, it is a relationship of purpose. When viewed with this perspective, we see the tremendous impact relationships of purpose can have on relationships of circumstance.

Because of some erroneous philosophies believed in the world, the level of relationships of purpose has been blurred almost beyond distinction. We will be looking at three types of philosophies that affect relationships of purpose later in this book. It is important to note that the view we hold regarding these philosophies will profoundly affect the way we approach relationships of purpose.

Because of the cacophony of voices clamoring for their own particular philosophy, we must carefully study what our responsibilities are when we choose to enter into relationships of purpose. Young people need to be taught those responsibilities before they make decisions that affect their lives and the lives of others for years to come. One decision with the potential to alter the future for young people is the decision to enter into a dating relationship.

Dating is a relationship of purpose because it begins with a choice and a goal. Even if the perceived purpose is simply to have fun, a bond is being established. Patterns of communication are developed. The transition from a simple relationship to a more complex relationship with increased responsibilities is almost imperceptible. Without knowing it or intending for it to happen, communication, upon which familiarity is based, is shared. The rules of the relationship and the attending responsibilities can change, and either one or both of the partners could find themselves unprepared to fulfill those responsibilities. The results can be devastating not only to the couple but to every other relationship in which they have a part.

If both partners in the dating relationship understand its purpose and its limits and stay within the preestablished bounds, dating can be a very rewarding experience. This is why it is so important for parents and their children to build positive, healthy relationships and for children to learn, before dating begins, how those relationships are established. If that is not done, the dating years can become a nightmare for the whole family. When guidelines for any relationship are not established beforehand or are ignored, many other relationships will be harmed for years to come.

The fallout from violating the rules in relationships of purpose affects many other relationships. Others are drawn into and are affected by the choices we make in relationships of purpose. This extends to relationships of circumstance and unfairly impacts individuals who have no choice in the establishment of the relationship but find themselves in positions of responsibility or in conflict situations not of their choosing.

To illustrate the ripple effect in relationships, consider again the sexual relationship. Many more individuals are involved in this relationship than the two individuals seeking self-gratification. Even if steps are taken to prevent conception, the sexual relationship, when performed outside of marriage, violates the rights and privileges of any future partner. Paul warned against such violation when he wrote:

> For this is the will of God, your sanctification;
> [that is] that you abstain from sexual immorality; that
> each of you know how to possess his own vessel in
> sanctification and honor, not in lustful passion, like

the Gentiles who do not know God; [and] that no man transgress and defraud his brother in the matter because the Lord is [the] avenger in all these things, just as we also told you before and solemnly warned [you.]. (1 Thessalonians 4:3–6)

From this we see that engaging in sex outside of marriage is a fraudulent act that robs someone else of what is due him or her. For the Christian, a sexual relationship outside of marriage also violates the relationship between the Christian and the Lord Jesus Christ. Concerning this we read:

Do you not know that your bodies are members of Christ? Shall I then take away the members of Christ and make them members of a harlot? May it never be! Or do you not know that the one who joins himself to a harlot is one body [with her?] For He says, "THE TWO SHALL BECOME ONE FLESH." But the one who joins himself to the Lord is one spirit [with Him.] Flee immorality. Every [other] sin that a man commits is outside the body, but the immoral man sins against his own body. (1 Corinthians 6:15–18)

Teaching young people how to enter into relationships of purpose, how to establish the goals and limits of those relationships, and how to stick to the preestablished rules of those relationships is critical in this day of personal freedom, free-sex, and alternative lifestyles. If one of the participants in the relationship of purpose does not hold to the same values as the other, the relationship becomes selfish and abusive and can lead to heartache for years to come and even for the rest of one's life.

One of the important questions to ask yourself before deciding to enter into a relationship of purpose is, "Do I have the resources to fulfill my responsibilities in this relationship?" These types of relationships usually begin with some form of contract, either written or oral. Relationships of purpose always require a change in our lives. Are we willing to make those changes? Will we be happy with the changes once they are made? Often we cannot go back to where we were before we entered the relationship. Therefore, it is very important to consider all aspects of the relationship before moving ahead.

Relationships of purpose also involve a commitment of time. Do we have the time to fulfill our obligations in the relationship? Are we willing to stay with the relationship for the agreed upon time, until we have fulfilled our responsibilities in it? Considering the time commitment is especially vital when entering into long-term relationships, such as marriage, or when assuming the role of a parent. These relationships last a lifetime.

Level 3: Relationships of Fulfillment

The third level of relationships is relationships of fulfillment. These are relationships that may have begun as either relationships of circumstance or relationships of purpose and, through time, bring personal fulfillment and enrichment to our lives. Not all relationships of circumstance or purpose become relationships of fulfillment. Simply accomplishing a goal or fulfilling a contract does not produce this kind of fulfillment in life. Fulfillment is richer and deeper. Relationships of fulfillment take time, energy, and personal attention.

Over time, conflicts arise in any relationship. Not all conflicts are due to sin. Some conflicts may simply be differences of opinion, preference, or goals. Even when the conflict does not begin as sin, if the conflict is not managed well, it will most certainly result in sin by individuals on one or both sides of the conflict.

A relationship of fulfillment is one in which the parties have learned to work through the conflicts to achieve a common goal for mutual benefit. These could also be called relationships of achievement. However, not all relationships that achieve an end can be characterized as relationships of fulfillment. The difference is that some relationships achieve goals that do not produce fulfillment. For instance, paying off a five-year contract on a vehicle might bring a sense of accomplishment, yet, in the end, we are left with a worn-out car that needs to be replaced. The fulfillment discussed here is the joy of being able to accomplish a goal together and to enjoy the benefits of that accomplishment together. To accomplish such a goal, those involved in the relationship might have to change, to exert effort, to expend personal resources and time, to give and take. In the example of buying a car, the benefit to the relationship while together achieving that goal will last long after the car is worn out and gone. When we reach the level of fulfillment in one relationship, we are better able to reach the level of fulfillment in others. This is why it is important to teach these principles to our children early, so that they can begin to develop the skills that will help them lay a foundation for relationships of fulfillment for the rest of their lives. Paul wrote:

> Instruct those who are rich in this present world not to be conceited or to fix their hope on the uncertainty of riches, but on God, who richly supplies us with all things to enjoy. [Instruct them] to do good, to be rich in good works, to be generous and ready to share, storing up for themselves the treasure of a good foundation for the future, so that they may take hold of that which is life indeed. (1 Timothy 6:17–19)

The world teaches that fulfillment comes through acquiring material wealth. Instead, fulfillment comes through meeting the needs of others. Learning to serve others is the best foundation we can possibly lay for the future. In the last sentence of the preceding passage, Paul used a phrase that could be translated "fulfillment" when he described the goal: to "take hold of that which is life indeed." A paraphrase in today's vernacular could be "Man, that's really living!"

Some relationships of purpose never reach the level of fulfillment because there are roadblocks that frustrate those who are involved in the relationships. Sometimes a lack of fulfillment occurs when expectations are too high or there is a failure to understand the relationship before entering into it. Other times, a lack of fulfillment could be due to a change in circumstances beyond our control: a failed business venture, a drop in the stock market, loss of a job, accidents, or failing health. Yet the new circumstances do not automatically absolve us of our responsibilities. Nor do the new circumstances mean that achieving fulfillment is not possible. What these usually mean is that we are forced to work together to adjust to the changing circumstances. When we are able to do that, our mutual achievements in overcoming obstacles are what bring the greatest fulfillment in our relationships. This is why James wrote:

> Consider it all joy, my brethren, when you encounter various trials, knowing that the testing of your faith produces endurance. And let endurance have [its] perfect result, that you may be perfect and complete, lacking in nothing. (James 1:2–4)

The greatest glory to God is when we obtain fulfillment in our relationships based on wise decisions and our faith in Christ. This is true when we learn to walk in the Spirit individually and corporately and to apply His Word to our relationships. In Galatians 5:16, we are exhorted to "walk by the Spirit." [2] This refers to individuals making each decision in life under the control and direction of the Holy Spirit. In Galatians 5:25, we are exhorted to "walk by the Spirit." [3] Here, the meaning is to march together like soldiers marching in rank. This refers to walking corporately, keeping in step with each other while the Holy Spirit, through the Word of God, calls cadence.

Forgiveness is also an important factor in achieving fulfillment in our relationships. When we offend each other, we weaken our relationship with each other. When we forgive each other and come to the place of genuine reconciliation, then the relationship becomes stronger than it was before the conflict. If we refuse to forgive or to seek forgiveness and reconciliation with each other, then we not only weaken that relationship but also diminish our ability to achieve fulfillment in other relationships. We establish a pattern of unforgiveness. We become irreconcilable (Cf. 2 Timothy 3:3).

Relationships of fulfillment are based upon our freedom in Christ and not upon rules and regulations. It is important to understand the context of Galatians 5. The Book of Galatians was written to refute the false teachers who came after the apostle Paul and who were teaching that a person had to keep the law to be saved. Many today falsely teach that relationships must be based upon law. Paul corrected that when he stated that laws are for children too young to know how to make correct choices (Cf. Galatians 4:1–3). Those who accept Christ as Savior, and who thereby receive the indwelling Holy Spirit, are set free from the law as a means of controlling their behavior. Instead, they should choose to walk in the Spirit and allow the Spirit to dictate their behavior. The Holy Spirit will never lead us to choose to do that which is unlawful. That is what it means to live above the law (Cf. Galatians 5:18, 5:23b).

Fulfillment in a relationship can only be achieved through the power of the Holy Spirit. The Holy Spirit helps us to take our minds off ourselves and to choose to serve others in that relationship. This is probably the greatest failure of meism. A self-centered person does not see himself or herself as serving others. He or she is only thinking about self and self-gratification. On the other hand, walking in the Spirit enables us to come to a place of selflessness. Paul writes:

> For you were called to freedom, brethren; only [do] not [turn] your freedom into an opportunity for the flesh, but through love serve one another. For the whole Law is fulfilled in one word, in the [statement] "YOU SHALL LOVE YOUR NEIGHBOR AS YOURSELF." (Galatians 5:13–14)

It is important to teach and model the lifestyle of walking in the Spirit to our children and to new believers. A lack of understanding in this area leaves many people frustrated and empty because they do not achieve fulfillment in their relationships.

Relationships of fulfillment are not only fulfilling to those of us involved in relationships here on earth; they are also fulfilling to God the Father. As a part of His vineyard, we are now bearing the fruit of righteousness as branches of His vine (John 15:1*ff*). Those relationships are also fulfilling to the angels who surround the throne of God. And they are fulfilling to Jesus because His death on the cross for us is bearing fruit in our lives.

PUTTING RESPONSIBILITY BACK INTO RELATIONSHIPS

While we will not achieve fulfillment in every relationship, both relationships of circumstance and relationships of purpose have the potential of reaching the level of fulfillment. Whether a relationship is one of circumstance or purpose, we must consider our responsibilities in the relationship in order for it to succeed. We will never achieve fulfillment in our relationships until we fulfill our responsibilities.

When I accepted Christ as my savior, I entered into a relationship of purpose with Jesus Christ. He promised to save me and He did. However, I did not understand some of my responsibilities in this relationship, so there were many times when I did not hold up my part of the bargain. Please understand that I use this colloquialism knowing that my salvation was by grace and grace alone. The relationship with Jesus Christ, which my salvation brought me, involved responsibilities on my part of which I was not aware.

Two years after my decision to receive Christ as my Savior, several individuals questioned my salvation because of my lifestyle. I still had some of the bad habits I had acquired before I entered into this relationship of purpose. In the beginning, I was concerned about my eternal destiny. I did not want to go to hell. I had a whole list of things I wanted Jesus to do for me, but I did not understand what He wanted from me. John spelled out one of those when he wrote, "And you know that He appeared in order to take away sins; and in Him there is no sin" (1 John 3:5). Paul added, "For you have been bought with a price: therefore glorify God in your body" (1 Corinthians 6:20).

Here we see an important principle governing relationships, particularly relationships of purpose. Very quickly we may encounter personal responsibilities that we never anticipated. This is why it is so important to stop and consider what might lie ahead when we choose to enter into relationships of purpose. Once the choice has been made, we assume the obligation to fulfill our responsibilities in the relationship, even if we did not know what those responsibilities were before we chose to enter into it. Failure to meet those responsibilities means a failed relationship.

Marriage begins as a relationship of purpose. Most of us enter into marriage hoping our partner will meet our needs. But our greater concern should be whether or not we will be able to fulfill our responsibilities to meet our partner's needs. Paul pointed this out when he wrote:

> Now concerning the things about which you wrote, it is good for a man not to touch a woman. But because of immoralities, let each man have his own wife, and let each woman have her own husband. Let the husband fulfill his *duty* to his wife, and likewise also the wife to her husband. The wife does not have *authority* over her own body, but the husband [does;] and likewise also the husband does not have *authority* over his own body, but the wife [does.] Stop depriving one another, except by agreement for a time that you may devote yourselves to prayer, and come together again lest Satan tempt you because of your lack of self-control. (1 Corinthians 7:1–5, italics mine)

Notice the little words *duty* and *authority* in this section. One time, I was teaching this passage to an adult Sunday school class. After class, an older woman came up to me and said she was offended by the terms *duty* and *authority*. She said that if her husband ever said it was her duty, she would tell him to get lost. No amount of explanation could persuade her to change her attitude.

This is true of so many individuals who enter into relationships of purpose without forethought or who rebel against the teaching of God's Word. Sometimes, we have nothing left to hold on to in a relationship other than our duty. The trials of life can rob us of the joy of a relationship. Interpersonal conflicts can rob us of joy. But when we work through those conflicts to the mutual benefit of each other and forgive the offenses committed and achieve true reconciliation, then we enter into a new level of experience in the relationship. It becomes a relationship of fulfillment.

When it is possible to reach fulfillment in a relationship, we need to do it. Failure to do so will affect every other relationship. Peter made this clear when he exhorted:

> You husbands likewise, live with [your wives] in an understanding way, as with a weaker vessel, since she is a woman; and grant her honor as a fellow heir of the grace of life, so that your prayers may not be hindered. (1 Peter 3:7)

Failure to achieve fulfillment in marriage means failure in our relationship with God. John made a similar point when he wrote, "If someone says, 'I love God,' and hates his brother, he is a liar; for the one who does not love his brother whom he has seen, cannot love God whom he has not seen" (1 John 4:20).

There is one final thought regarding relationships of fulfillment before we conclude this section. Remember our discussion earlier with regard to Jesus' trip through Samaria and John's statement that He had to go through Samaria? We noted that the Greek term *deo* in the context means "divine appointment." We find this term again in another unique context. The situation involved conflicts among church members at Corinth, particularly in the way they were observing the Lord's supper. Paul wrote:

> But in giving this instruction, I do not praise you, because you come together not for the better but for the worse. For, in the first place, when you come together as a church, I hear that divisions exist among you; and in part I believe it. *For there must also be* factions among you, in order that those who are approved may have become evident among you. (1 Corinthians 11:17–19, italics mine).

Notice the phrase in the last sentence, "For there must also be." This translates the same Greek term, *deo*, found in the passage regarding the woman at the well. Here it has the same meaning, "Divine appointment." Does that mean that God is behind many of the conflicts in churches today? I believe, when we understand it in the right way, the answer is yes. God allows conflict to come into our lives to mature us. This is what James meant when he wrote that trials make us "... perfect and complete, lacking in nothing" (James 1:4).

In the Old Testament, God repeatedly warned Israel that violation of His law would bring conflict with their neighbors. In the Book of Proverbs we read, "When a man's ways are pleasing to the LORD, He makes even his enemies to be at peace with him" (Proverbs 16:7). In another passage we read:

> Then God sent an evil spirit between Abimelech and the men of Shechem; and the men of Shechem dealt treacherously with Abimelech, in order that the violence done to the seventy sons of Jerubbaal might come, and their blood might be laid on Abimelech their brother, who killed them, and on the men of Shechem, who strengthened his hands to kill his brothers. (Judges 9:23–24)

From this we see that failure to respect others in our relationships and failure to act responsibly may lead God to intervene and bring back upon us the results of our failure.

In the passage in 1 Corinthians 11, Paul told the Corinthians that God was at work in their midst allowing conflicts in order to sift them so that He could produce a cleansed and pure church. This does not mean that we should set out to stir up trouble so the church can be purified. Nor does it mean that we are automatically the approved ones simply because we believe we are right and others are wrong. What it means is that

God is personally involved in our lives and the life of the church. Therefore, we need to take care, lest we find ourselves in opposition to Him and what He is trying to accomplish. Church conflicts can be opportunities to enter into new and more fulfilling relationships than would be possible without the conflicts. This is true provided we apply the Scriptures to our lives and walk in the Spirit as He commands.

It is a sad commentary on our society that so many individuals never achieve the level of fulfillment in relationships that God intends. And in this regard, Christians do not have a much better track record. Christians experience almost as many divorces as the general population. Some churches fail to reach the level of fulfillment in relationships. Many individuals become fearful of relationships altogether. Failure breeds failure. America is becoming a society marked by failed relationships. With increasing speed and magnitude, each succeeding generation becomes more dysfunctional than the generation before. If we do not put on the breaks and turn around, we will surely be facing chaos in the streets. Some might say we have already reached that point when children are killing children in our nation's public schools.

I pray to our Heavenly Father that this book will lead many to answers on how to help turn the tide. If God chooses not to allow the tide to turn, and He may do that, at least you who are reading this book might find answers in God's Word to help you improve the relationships in your life.

BUILDING RELATIONSHIPS BIBLICALLY

There is an important principle that I live by and try to convey to those I teach. It is the principle that I do not go back and examine past decisions in light of present knowledge. Before deciding to enter into relationships of purpose, I seek God's will from a study of His Word, I seek wise counsel, and I sit down and count the cost. Then I make the decision. I make the decision with the attitude that it is God's will for my life. Many times, things do not work out the way I expect, even when I weigh the issues carefully beforehand. If I sought His counsel on the matter and trusted Him to provide the wisdom I needed to make the decision and to provide the resources to fulfill my obligations in that relationship, I cannot go back to the starting point where I was before I made the decision. I am obligated to fulfill my part of the bargain. The passage of Scripture I base this on is James 1:2–8:

> Consider it all joy, my brethren, when you encounter various trials, knowing that the testing of your faith produces endurance. And let endurance have [its] perfect result, that you may be perfect and complete, lacking in nothing. But if any of you lacks wisdom, let him ask of God, who gives to all men generously and without reproach, and it will be given to him. But he must ask in faith without any doubting, for the one who doubts is like the surf of the sea, driven and tossed by the wind. For let not that man expect that he will receive anything from the Lord, [being] a double-minded man, unstable in all his ways.

In applying this passage to the present discussion, the trials represent those unforeseen conflicts that arise from the decisions I made when I entered into a relationship of purpose. Whenever we enter into a relationship of purpose, we are agreeing to certain obligations. In a sense, we are obligating God as well, since we are placing our trust in Him to give us the ability to fulfill our responsibilities.

If we have done our homework before entering into the relationship, and if things do not turn out the way we planned, we have the assurance that the trial is from God and His purpose in allowing the trial is for our good. It is an opportunity to cry out to God for wisdom regarding the trial and to rest in the assurance that He will work everything out according to His honor and glory.

Many enter into relationships of purpose without considering the responsibilities and consequences of those relationships and without seeking God's will. Then, when things go wrong, they blame God. When they do so, they become double-minded and unstable because of their own failure. Their troubles are compounded when they go back and examine those decisions in the light of present knowledge and fail to acknowledge their own culpability in bringing those trials upon themselves.

As we have seen before, one of the most important relationships of purpose we can enter into is marriage. We do not know and cannot know all of the ramifications of this decision when we make it. Yet we can make such a decision with confidence through seeking God's will in His Word, through the leading of the Holy Spirit, and through listening to wise counsel. Confidence does not guarantee that things will always work out according to our expectation. Many times, they will not. Any time we enter into long-term relationships of purpose, we do not know in advance what the end will be. But when we experience trials, we can have a clear conscience that the trials are not the result of a failure on our part. It may be that God intended all along to allow a different outcome than we expected for our good. To those who enter into relationships of purpose responsibly, God has promised, "And we know that God causes all things to work together for good to those who love God, to those who are called according to [His] purpose (Romans 8:28).

Jesus is called "the Alpha and Omega" because He knows the beginning, the end, and everything in between (Revelation 1:8; 21:6; 22:13). Even though we do not know what the future will bring, He does. When entering into relationships of purpose, faith in Him is absolutely imperative. Prayer is vital as well. John wrote:

> And the witness is this, that God has given us eternal life, and this life is in His Son. He who has the Son has the life; he who does not have the Son of God does not have the life. These things I have written to you who believe in the name of the Son of God, in order that you may know that you have eternal life. And this is the confidence which we have before Him, that, if we ask anything according to His will, He hears us. And if we know that He hears us [in]

whatever we ask, we know that we have the requests which we have asked from Him. (1 John 5:11–15)

Notice that John was writing to individuals who "believe in the name of the Son of God." Since they believe, they must also have the Son. If they have the Son, they must also have eternal life. Eternal life is a quality relationship with God that will last for eternity. So why did John have to write and tell them they have eternal life? Because things can happen in our relationship with God—in this context, it is called *sin*—that disrupt the enjoyment of that relationship. It is possible to have a relationship with God and not feel like we have it, because of the barriers that we have allowed to come between us and God. This is also true of our relationship with each other, whether it is a relationship of circumstance or of purpose.

The good news is that, even though we do not know what barriers may come in the future that might hinder our relationships, we still can enter with confidence because Jesus is the Alpha and Omega. Nothing will surprise Him. When we do our homework and examine our relationships of purpose before we enter into them, when we commit ourselves to fulfilling our responsibilities in all of our relationships, and when we put our trust in Christ, then we do not have to look back with regret, even if barriers do come and we are not able to reach fulfillment. We can pray about these barriers and ask God to do His will, either by helping us to overcome the barriers or by helping us to learn to live with them. Then, even if God does not answer the prayers the way we want Him to, we still can have the assurance that our prayers are being answered according to His will.

THE NEED FOR TRUTH IN RELATIONSHIPS

Building godly relationships is possible only when both parties in the relationship are committed to truth. This seems so basic that we often overlook this important aspect of building relationships. Yet is this not the very thing that destroyed relationships in the Garden of Eden? The first thing that happened was that the truth of God's Word was called into question. Then a lie was told about that truth. Finally, the truth itself was ignored altogether and Adam and Eve attempted to build their relationship upon a lie. We will be looking at this matter in depth later on. Here it must be underscored. Any attempt to build a relationship must begin by laying a foundation of truth.

The illustration of the wise man who built his house upon a rock is familiar to many. It is found in Matthew 7:24–29. Luke recorded a similar illustration that Jesus taught, but the details and application are different.

> Why do you call Me, "Lord, Lord," and do not do what I say? Everyone who comes to Me and hears My words and acts on them, I will show you whom he is like: he is like a man building a house, who dug deep and laid a foundation upon the rock; and when a flood rose, the torrent burst against that house and could not shake it, because it had been well built.

But the one who has heard and has not acted [accordingly], is like a man who built a house upon the ground without any foundation; and the torrent burst against it and immediately it collapsed, and the ruin of that house was great. (Luke 6:46–49)

As with the illustration in Matthew's Gospel, the rock here is Jesus Christ, who calls Himself "the way, the truth, and the life" (John 14:6). We need to establish all of our relationships upon the foundation of the truth of God. Only then can we ever expect to achieve fulfillment in those relationships.

AVOID US-AND-THEM THINKING

We have seen that the goal in our relationships is to reach the third level: fulfillment. We have also seen that it may not be possible, either because of the kind of relationship it is or because of a failure on the part of others in that relationship. Often this lack of fulfillment leads us to feel as if we do not have a relationship with the people with whom we are involved and, therefore, we do not have any responsibilities to them. In turn, this can lead to an us-and-them attitude. Us-and-them thinking occurs when we begin to focus on what divides us more than what unites us.

When delineating principles of conflict management, most agree that there cannot be any effective solutions to conflicts without first recognizing that there is a valued relationship between the opposing sides in the conflict. Whether we are religious or secular, Christian or some other religion, if we engage in us-and-them thinking, we will never be able to work together to find solutions to our problems. When we embrace faulty views about our relationships with each other, we undermine the very fabric of society and perpetuate hatred in society.

We do not have to agree on every aspect of life in order to agree upon solutions to the conflicts. It was not differences of race, ethnicity, or even religion that produced the disastrous results seen at Columbine High. It was a failure to see what unites us as members of the human race. Whether we like it or not, we all live on this planet. We all are affected by the disfunctionality of society. The fact that we can now view conflicts in society anywhere in the world at any moment demonstrates how important it is to identify how we are related to each other and how we can use these relationships to change society for the better.

Historically, the Christian church has failed society by engaging in us-and-them thinking. This has caused the church to fail in delivering its message, in presenting the gospel of peace, and in accomplishing its mission of bringing people together to serve a risen Savior. The fact that there is one human race is evident everywhere in the Bible. Therefore, there is solidarity among all races and ethnic groups regardless of religious persuasion. We are related. Jesus referred to this solidarity when He commanded His disciples:

> You have heard that it was said, "YOU SHALL LOVE YOUR NEIGHBOR and hate your enemy." But I say to you,

love your enemies, and pray for those who perse-
cute you in order that you may be sons of your Father who is in heaven; for He causes His sun to rise
on [the] evil and [the] good, and sends rain on [the]
righteous and [the] unrighteous. (Matthew 5:43–45)

Paul taught this solidarity when he referred to ". . . the
kindness of God our Savior and [His] love for mankind . . ." (Titus 3:4). This is a beautiful word picture in
the Greek language in which it was written. The phrase
"love for mankind" translates one Greek word, *philanthropia*. This term is made up of two words, *philos* meaning "love," and *anthropia* referring to the human race. It
is transliterated into the English language as *philan-
thropy*. More is going to be said about the Greek term
philos in the last section of this book. Here, it is helpful
to see that philanthropia is an attitude of warmth and
affection for the human race. How would history over
the past two thousand years have been changed if the
Christian church had always had this attitude toward
all mankind?

It is interesting that most systematic theology books
have a section titled "Anthropology." In theology, anthropology is a systematic study of what the Bible
teaches regarding the human race. Usually, authors
emphasize the differences of opinion among scholars
regarding views of the human race and seldom mention the similarities of opinion. So far, most anthropolo-
gists believe there is only one human race. What would
happen if we all listed our areas of agreement and for-

got for a moment the areas where we disagree? Perhaps it would be possible to arrive at some agreement that we are all related and, because of that relationship, to come to some agreement regarding the social issues we all face. Together, we could discover some solutions that would benefit us all.

Given God's attitude of loving affection toward the human race and the command given to Christians to love every member of the human race (even loving our enemies as God loves them), every Christian should be a philanthropist in the true meaning of that word. As God blesses all of us by causing the sun to shine and the rain to fall upon everyone, so Christians should seek to provide the basic necessities of life to everyone as much as possible (Matthew 5:45).

Paul underscored this same thought when he commanded the churches, "So then, while we have opportunity, let us do good to all men, and especially to those who are of the household of the faith" (Galatians 6:10). From this verse, we see that even though our first responsibility is to take care of the household of faith, we still have a responsibility to all people. This implies that we are related to every other member of the human race and, therefore, share in the responsibility to participate in caring for the needs of the human race.

In another passage, we find that the human race shares something else in common: All men have been created in the image of God. Because of this, we need to be careful what we say about each other and how we communicate with each other. James wrote:

> So also the tongue is a small part of the body, and [yet] it boasts of great things. Behold, how great a forest is set aflame by such a small fire! And the tongue is a fire, the [very] world of iniquity; the tongue is set among our members as that which defiles the entire body, and sets on fire the course of [our] life, and is set on fire by hell. For every species of beasts and birds, of reptiles and creatures of the sea, is tamed, and has been tamed by the human race. But no one can tame the tongue; [it is] a restless evil [and] full of deadly poison. With it we bless [our] Lord and Father, and with it we curse men, who have been made in the likeness of God. (James 3:5–9)

This leads us to something else we need if we are going to be a part of the solution and not a part of the problem in society. We need to learn how to communicate with each other in every relationship, whether or not the relationship reaches the level of fulfillment. In fact, we will never achieve a relationship of fulfillment without first becoming an effective communicator in that relationship.

CHAPTER TWO

Communication: The Key
to Building Relationships

We often hear that we live in the Age of Communication. Western culture is founded upon the rapid and broad dissemination of information. The telephone, radio, television, computers, and other technological advances link individuals, homes, and businesses. The advent of the Internet, fiber optics, and satellites has made it possible to access information from around the world in microseconds. However, all of these advances in technology have not made us better communicators. At times, technology actually impedes communication because individuals hold a false view of what genuine communication is. Communication is not the relaying of data from one machine to another. While we might borrow terminology from the communication industry, unless human responsibility is expressed through relationships, there is no genuine communication. The inverse is also true. Relationships are not possible without effective communication.

The term *communication* derives from a Latin root meaning "to impart," "share," or "to make common." Recently, with the advancement of technology, the definition of communication has evolved to where it merely refers to the transfer of ones and zeroes—the binary language of computers. While computers can transfer a phenomenal amount of data, they are only tools and cannot communicate in the true sense of the word. From here on in this book, *communication* means the transfer of a message from one individual or group of individuals to another individual or group. It also means there has been a response and a corresponding change in the relationship between the two individuals or groups.

In the first chapter of this book, we identified three levels of relationships: relationships of circumstance, relationships of purpose, and relationships of fulfillment. In order to move from relationships of circumstance and purpose to relationships of fulfillment, we must identify and carry out our God-given responsibilities. In order to do that, we must be able to communicate with others in those relationships, whether we are seeking to fulfill our responsibilities to them or they are seeking to fulfill theirs to us.

WHAT IS THE MESSAGE AND WHO IS RESPONSIBLE FOR IT?

Our goal should be to build healthy relationships, relationships of fulfillment. This can be accomplished by learning how to communicate effectively. Communication is not simply talking. Communication involves transmitting and receiving a message in a way that allows an appropriate response from the one receiving the message. This message is not necessarily couched in audible sounds. In fact, it is possible to say one thing but communicate an entirely different message than what was said. Many messages are transferred visually through body language. Communication has not taken place until there is a change in attitude and/or behavior.

TELLING IS NOT COMMUNICATING

Young people are often blamed for bad behavior and are reminded that they have been told over and over not to engage in such behavior. However, telling is not communicating. They may, in fact, have received the true message behind the telling. It might have been "Do as I say, not as I do" or some other message that annulled or altered the message spoken.

We see several examples of saying one thing but doing another in the Sermon on the Mount in Matthew 5. Jesus presents five topics that were popular teaching points of the religious leaders. A careful overview of those five topics demonstrates that the reason so many were not getting the message was because the religious leaders were saying one thing but doing another. The section begins with Jesus denouncing the scribes and Pharisees:

> Do not think that I came to abolish the Law or the Prophets; I did not come to abolish but to fulfill. For truly I say to you, until heaven and earth pass away, not the smallest letter or stroke shall pass away from the Law, until all is accomplished. Whoever then annuls one of the least of these commandments, and so

teaches others, shall be called least in the kingdom of heaven; but whoever keeps and teaches [them], he shall be called great in the kingdom of heaven. For I say to you, that unless your righteousness surpasses [that] of the scribes and Pharisees, you shall not enter the kingdom of heaven. (Matthew 5:17–20)

The scribes were experts in the Law of Moses. Like many lawyers today, they were experts in how to get around the law instead of how to obey it. The Pharisees were the moralists who took it upon themselves to judge everyone else's behavior but made excuses for their own behavior. What follows are five examples of how those religious lawyers and moralists taught the Law but found ways to avoid the moral requirements themselves.

The five topics include the law against committing murder, the law against adultery, the law against making false promises, the law requiring restitution, and a supposed law teaching the sons of Israel to hate their enemies. In each law, the scribes and Pharisees found ways to get around the moral underpinnings so as to make themselves look righteous in the eyes of men while at the same time violating those laws.

Jesus confronted them on each issue. What good is a law against murder if we destroy others with our angry tempers? What good is a law against adultery if we slobber all over pornography, laugh at dirty jokes, and destroy the sacred bond of marriage by divorcing our marriage partner? What good is a law against making false promises if we cheat on our income tax and steal from our employers by pilfering and failing to do honest work? What good is the law of restitution if we become angry when someone else steps on our personal rights and we have no regard for the rights of others or for laws meant to protect us from each other? Many religious zealots ascribe to false teachings of hate toward others, often toward those whose only "fault" is a different color of skin, a different race, a different religion, a different economic bracket, or a different language. Where in God's Word does He ever teach us to hate those who are different from us or those who are our enemies? Nowhere.

The problems in society will not be overcome until we adults—we parents—stop teaching one thing with our mouths and another by our attitudes and actions. Our children are watching us. We are teaching them even when we do not mean to. Children do not mirror the attitude and behavior of their parents; they magnify them, especially the faults. The messages we teach through our attitudes and behaviors come through loud and clear to our children and often drown out the messages we think we are conveying verbally.

When I was growing up back on the farm, much of the work was performed by hired hands. Some of the work was seasonal, so there was a constant stream of workers coming and going. One summer, several workers were hired to help with the pea harvest. One day, some military police came looking for a man who was AWOL. They arrested one of the workers. The car he was driving was impounded because it and much of its contents were stolen. They left the vehicle in the care of my father with instructions to turn it over to the county sheriff when he came for it. The car was towed to the barnyard behind our house and left there for more than a week.

During that time, I was looking for some tools in the tool shed and ran across some strange items among the tools: a Geiger counter, a large flashlight, and other items I had not seen before. A few days after the sheriff retrieved the car, some investigators came back. I was working in a field near the road and my father was on the other side of the field near the river. The investigators stopped me and asked if I had seen a Geiger counter and a large flashlight. Immediately, I knew what had happened. I lied and told them I had not seen those items.

Later, after the officers left, my father came to where I was working and asked me what they wanted. I told him they were looking for items that had been removed from the stolen car. He asked me what I told them, and I repeated to him the answer I gave them. He said, "Good boy," and complimented me on the lie I had just told to the authorities to protect him. It was one of the few compliments I ever received from him. Later that day, I went back to see if the items were still in the tool shed. They had been removed.

My adopted parents were pillars in the community, looked up to by many, and were generous when it came to helping individuals and families in need. However, such incidents made it very difficult for me to hear the message I am sure they tried to communicate to me: that a good citizen of the community is honest and trustworthy.

The problem is not that adults make mistakes. Our children know when we make mistakes. The problem is we refuse to acknowledge our mistakes. In this way we try to teach one thing to our children and do another ourselves. It is then that we communicate loud and clear the wrong message.

One day, Jesus was teaching His disciples regarding setting a good example:

> And he said to His disciples, "It is inevitable that stumbling blocks should come, but woe to him through whom they come! It would be better for him if a millstone were hung around his neck and he were thrown into the sea, than that he should cause one of these little ones to stumble." (Luke 17:1–2)

Parenting is an awesome responsibility. It is complicated today by all of the hype and hoopla of sports, entertainment, and the merchandising of toys and games. It is difficult to tell what is real and what is computer generated. Added to this are the lies and half-truths many government leaders tell, and the propaganda of single-agenda political activists who overstate the truth of their position while denying the truth of their opponent's position. It is a wonder any moral truth ever filters down to the next generation. In fact, it is obvious from the behavior of many children today that moral truth is not being taught. We are reaping the fruit of all of this false communication.

The home and family should be the one place where a child can find genuine concern, safety, and truth. Yet with so many parents divorcing and then using their children as Ping-Pong balls in their personal vendettas, there is little doubt why so many young people today have lost their way.

THE MESSAGE NEEDS READY RECEPTORS

Duplicity—saying one thing but meaning another—on the part of adults is not the only cause of the downhill slide that society has taken over the last several years. Children also bear some of the responsibility. There are parents who are doing their best with what they have. Many parents did not have good role models themselves because their parents were caught up in war protests, free speech, free love, or substance abuse. Their parents did not have time to learn how to be good parents or to teach their children how to be parents. For the most part, in the relay race of life, those of Generation X who are now parents did not drop the baton of morality. It was dropped by the previous generation. Many of Generation X lost the race before they entered it.

How does a generation without role models get turned around? Toward the end of His three-and-a-half-year ministry, the moral teachers of Israel exasperated Jesus. In chapter 23 of Matthew's Gospel we read:

> Then Jesus spoke to the multitudes and to His disciples, saying: "The scribes and the Pharisees have seated themselves in the chair of Moses; *therefore all that they tell you, do and observe, but do not do according to their deeds; for* they say [things], and do not do [them.] And they tie up heavy loads, and lay them on men's

shoulders; but they themselves are unwilling to move them with [so much as] a finger. But they do all their deeds to be noticed by men; for they broaden their phylacteries, and lengthen the tassels [of their garments.] And they love the place of honor at banquets, and the chief seats in the synagogues, and respectful greetings in the market places, and being called by men, Rabbi." (Matthew 23:1–7, italics mine)

Here we see that the student is going to be held responsible for the lesson, even if the teacher does not live by what he teaches. When we see how far those religious leaders were from the truth, we might wonder why Jesus did not attack their teaching. In some places He did. Yet here Jesus placed the burden of sorting out truth from error, message from action, upon the shoulders of the learner because it was almost too late to change the teachers.

In the previous chapter, we discussed the need for truth as the foundation for healthy relationships. Here we see that we are going to be held responsible for truth whether or not the behavior of our teachers is consistent with the truth they teach. The message that needs to be transmitted is truth. Truth must be communicated from one generation to the next in order for society to survive. When our actions are consistent with truth, the message of truth is more easily transmitted. However, whether or not the one transmitting the truth behaves in a manner consistent with that truth, the next generation still has a responsibility to receive the message of truth.

Many today who are blaming the previous generation for their failures have lived as adults long enough to be responsible for their own actions. As a fifty-seven-year-old adult, I cannot blame my biological parents for my failures in life. I cannot blame my adopted parents for my failures in life either. My years from birth to the age of eight seem like a lifetime. My years from the age of eight, when I was adopted, to the age of seventeen, when I found myself on my own, seem like another lifetime. However, all those years combined make up only about one third of my life. At some point, I have to assume responsibility for my own behavior and accept the consequences when I am wrong.

Accepting responsibility for my own actions and asking for forgiveness for my failures was not something I learned from my adopted parents. Many times, I longed to hear them say one simple statement: "I was wrong. Please forgive me." But I never heard it. My children heard it from me frequently because I was determined not to make that mistake with them. A constant fear when raising my own children was that I would be that proverbial pendulum swinging too far the other direction, so as to become legalistic, authoritarian, and judgmental. I wanted them to know that I live with my own foibles daily, that I am not perfect, and that I am willing to confess to them my imperfections. Only they can say whether or not I was successful in conveying that truth.

Parenting is a partnership. It is a partnership between the parents and their children. No generation of parents has all the answers. No generation of children is totally irresponsible either. And yet what I hear while standing in checkout lines and in other places where parents and children gather is condescension from the parents toward their children, and a sarcastic, rebellious attitude on the part of children toward their parents. This has become the message communicated from one generation to the other. This is not healthy communication. In fact, it is a clear indication that communication has broken down almost totally between generations.

How Do We Communicate?

In this section, we want to consider the various tools we use to communicate. Some of these items will be referred to under other headings as well. Here, we are concerned about ways that society is beginning to destroy communication through critical and hypocritical attacks upon these basic tools.

We Communicate by Attitude

We communicate by our attitude. If our general attitude toward life is positive, the message we communicate is impacted positively by our attitude. If our general attitude toward life is negative, no matter how positive our words may be, they will be negatively impacted by our negative attitude. It is important that we listen to our inner thoughts to see what our general attitude is. If you are having difficulty conveying messages to others the way you intend for them to be conveyed, maybe your attitude is inconsistent with those messages.

The attitude of a man apart from Christ is limited to his own evaluation and opinion of information received through his five senses (See diagram 1). The result is a

DIAGRAM 1

Evaluation + Opinion = Attitude

strictly human view based solely on his ability to perceive correctly this information. On the other hand, the attitude of a Christian should consist of evaluation and opinion formed under the control of the Holy Spirit as He applies the knowledge of God's Word to the thought process. The result is what the Bible calls "the mind of Christ" (1 Corinthians 2:16) (See diagram 2).

It is easy to slip into a negative mindset today because most of what we hear in the media is negative. Bad news sells; good news does not. Society has been negatively impacted by the false philosophy of Existentialism. Existentialism begins with the premise that the world is absurd and promotes a depressing view of life. This negative philosophy permeates every facet of

DIAGRAM 2

God's Word

Evaluation + Opinion

The Holy Spirit

society today and conditions us to think negatively. We will discuss Existentialism in the next section.

Paul warned the church at Philippi about negative thinking. Considering the fact that he was incarcerated in Rome at the time the letter to Philippi was written, it is amazing that he did not go into an extended diatribe against the unjust Roman system or some unethical politician that might have added to his burden. Instead, the letter to the church at Philippi is one of the most positive of Paul's letters.

In commenting regarding the conflict among church members, he wrote, "Finally, brethren, whatever is true, whatever is honorable, whatever is right, whatever is pure, whatever is lovely, whatever is of good repute, if there is any excellence and if anything worthy of praise, let your mind dwell on these things" (Philippians 4:8). We need to be careful that negative things in life do not make us negative people. A person with a negative attitude will not help a situation and may even do great harm. A negative attitude hinders communication.

A number of years ago, I served as pastor of a church that was experiencing a lot of conflict. At the same time, one of the families in the church was experiencing serious personal problems. One of the problems was that the father in the household had been arrested for possession of an illegal substance. Part of his penalty was to be sent out of town for a period of time for rehabilitation. Many of us in the church were very concerned for him and his family and sought ways to support them through this crisis.

I encouraged the members of the church to keep in touch with him by correspondence, and some did. When I wrote, I was careful not to mention any of the problems in the church. However, a man in the church took it upon himself to send a material gift along with a letter in which he went into detail regarding all of the problems in the church. When the man returned from rehabilitation, what he remembered and appreciated most was not the material goods given to him by this man. It was the positive letters sent by those who did not feel he needed to know all of the negative things. The negative letter sent along with the gift nullified the good that could have otherwise been accomplished by the gift.

We need to learn to adjust our thinking so that we can communicate with each other out of attitudes that build one another up. There are times when we are justified in having a negative thought. However, negative thinking tears down the relationships we are trying to build. We can only build healthy relationships when we have a positive attitude.

Twice in the New Testament Paul refers to a drink offering: once in the letter to the church at Philippi in Philippians 2:17, and once to Timothy in 2 Timothy 4:6. In both contexts, he refers to the possibility that he might be put to death. The concept of a drink offering is taken from the Old Testament sacrificial system.

In the Law of Moses, every sacrifice was to be accompanied by a drink offering except the sacrifice for sin carried into the Holy of Holies each year on the Day of Atonement. The drink offering was wine that was poured out around the main sacrifice. In the culture of the Old Testament, wine represented joy and merriment. Therefore, the drink offering was a symbol of the joyful heart with which every sacrifice was to be offered. On the Day of Atonement, when the sacrifice offered by the high priest for his sins and the sins of the people was not accompanied by a drink offering, the message was that the offering was being presented with a broken and contrite heart.

In the New Testament, Christians offer sacrifices as well. These sacrifices are the testimonies we give regarding God's goodness to us and the good works we do for others in His name (Hebrews 13:15–16). If we have a negative attitude toward life, no matter how many good deeds we do in the name of Christ, and no matter how often we testify to His goodness to us, those sacrifices will be unacceptable to God because of our negative attitude. We must keep our eyes on Christ and learn to give thanks to God for everything because God causes all things to work together for good.

As society continues to be polarized by various factions and the dissemination of false philosophies, we must study God's Word to help cleanse our minds of the garbage that the world serves up constantly. In fact, we may even need to turn off the television and other forms of media once in a while so that we can hear the voice of God through His Word. Young people need to turn off and tune out the negative fare served up as entertainment. It is not entertainment if it conveys an attitude of contempt for others or promotes a negative attitude toward life. Constant feeding on the husks of the world will result in negativism and despair. Those kinds of attitudes prevent us from forming successful relationships. The only effective way to keep from developing a negative attitude is to fill our minds with the positive truths of Scripture.

We Communicate by Words

James wrote:

> Let not many [of you] become teachers, my brethren, knowing that as such we shall incur a stricter judgment. For we all stumble in many

[ways.] If anyone does not stumble in what he says, he is a perfect man, able to bridle the whole body as well. Now if we put the bits into the horses' mouths so that they may obey us, we direct their entire body as well. Behold, the ships also, though they are so great and are driven by strong winds, are still directed by a very small rudder, wherever the inclination of the pilot desires. So also the tongue is a small part of the body, and [yet] it boasts of great things. Behold, how great a forest is set aflame by such a small fire! And the tongue is a fire, the [very] world of iniquity; the tongue is set among our members as that which defiles the entire body, and sets on fire the course of [our] life, and is set on fire by hell. For every species of beasts and birds, of reptiles and creatures of the sea, is tamed, and has been tamed by the human race. But no one can tame the tongue; [it is] a restless evil [and] full of deadly poison. With it we bless [our] Lord and Father, and with it we curse men, who have been made in the likeness of God; from the same mouth come [both] blessing and cursing. My brethren, these things ought not to be this way. Does a fountain send out from the same opening [both] fresh and bitter [water?] Can a fig tree, my brethren, produce olives, or a vine produce figs? Nor [can] salt water produce fresh. (James 3:1–12)

Words are powerful tools in the hands of those who learn to use them skillfully. They can be used to convey every positive emotion known to man. They can also be used as brickbats to hurl at people. We need to be careful of the words we use, and we need to teach our children to be careful of the words they use. As James said, much damage is caused by carelessly speaking. Often, we find ourselves opening our mouths and inserting our feet. There is no good time for unguarded speech. This is why listening to dirty jokes is such a problem. They tend to stick in one's mind and are too easily regurgitated in an undisciplined moment.

Paul wrote, "Let no unwholesome word proceed from your mouth, but only such [a word] as is good for edification according to the need [of the] moment, that it may give grace to those who hear" (Ephesians 4:29). In another place he wrote, "Let your speech always be with grace, seasoned, as it were, with salt, so that you may know how you should respond to each person" (Colossians 4:6).

We must accept the responsibility for our words and their meanings, and we must accept the responsibility for the contexts in which the words are conveyed. Simply saying something may not convey our message at all or may communicate a distorted message if the context is not right. We must accept the responsibility of understanding the context of the person for whom the message is intended; or, if we are the receivers of the message, we must accept the responsibility of understanding the context of the person who sent the message. Effective communication cannot take place if we are insensitive to the circumstances in which we find the person with whom we are trying to communicate.

A pastor was called to the home of a woman whose husband died suddenly. The pastor was there to comfort her and to assist in planning the funeral service. As the widow related her sorrow to the pastor, his response was, "I understand."

This is a common response. However, this time the woman replied, "You don't understand. You can't understand." Clearly, this trite statement did not comfort this woman. We usually do not understand what the other person is thinking or feeling. Saying we do could be taken as insensitivity or a lack of sincerity on our part. Since hearing this illustration many years ago, I have tried to discipline myself in such situations to say, "I can appreciate," rather than, "I understand."

Children need to be taught the consequences of what they say. I am not a fisherman. My son, David, and I wanted to fish, but I lacked the ability to teach him. We decided to ask a friend who is a good fisherman to take us on one of his fishing trips. He and his wife arrived at the fishing area early and set up camp. He provided all the fishing tackle, boat, and gas. We set out early in the morning around sunup.

As the day wore on, even our friend was having difficulty snagging anything. The fish were not biting. After hours of sitting in the boat and catching nothing, I heard David let out a big sigh and complained, "This is boring!" My thoughts went immediately to our friend who had gone to great expense and was trying so hard to make our fishing trip successful. I shot back, "Boring is an unappreciative term. You should say, it is slow." David knew immediately he said the wrong thing. He has never forgotten that lesson regarding the use of inappropriate words.

It is interesting how free speech has come full circle in society. Thirty-years ago, many were demanding the right to say anything they wanted to say, no matter how vulgar or offensive. Today, many put themselves in the role of political-correctness police, whose purpose it is to stamp out any words they view as offensive, no matter what the meaning is behind them.

Political correctness is a tool of what has become known as *postmodernism*. Postmodernists, among other things, believe that "words don't *describe* reality, they *create* reality."[1] Space does not allow a full discussion of postmodernism. However, the full context of the above quote will help us understand some of the thinking in regard to the use of words.

A clear example of *constructivism* is how the political-correctness movement thrives on college campuses. Behind this movement is the supposition that the way we speak of others perpetuates a cultural climate of race and gender bias mythologies. The presumed key to doing away with those mythologies isn't challenging attitudes but talking differently. "Words don't *describe* reality; they *create* reality." We will never free society from such prejudices, they believe, until we control the language upon which those prejudices are based. Political correctness isn't just an attempt to keep from hurting people's feelings, but it's an attempt to change people by changing the cultural environment.[2]

We will be discussing the use of words in another context later on. Here, it is important to note that words are the first and perhaps most important aspect of communication. If the political-correctness police, or anyone else, succeed in undermining the importance of words to the communication process, not only will communication be more difficult, but relationships that depend upon effective communication will be undermined.

We Communicate by Body Language and Environmental Circumstances

It has been known for a long time that the context in which communication takes place has a lot to do with the effectiveness of that communication. When governments enter into negotiations with other governments, often the debate over the shape of the conference table becomes a stumbling block. It is possible to control the course of the meeting simply by where one sits at the table.

I was chairing a very contentious congregational meeting a few years ago. Since I had no advance warning that the meeting was going to take place, much less the contentious matters to be discussed, I did not have an opportunity to arrange the meeting hall in advance. Consequently, I found myself chairing the meeting from behind a large pulpit about three feet above the main floor of the meeting hall and several feet away from the front row. The meeting was a disaster. I could sense that every time I ruled from the chair, the ruling came down as an edict from on high. Without intending to convey it, many felt that I was being dictatorial. This was largely because of the configuration of the room in which the meeting took place.

Sometimes we need to accommodate the person with whom we are seeking to communicate by entering into their world. When my son, David, entered kindergarten, we visited the school and classroom and spoke at length with the person who was to be his teacher. We chose that particular teacher because she had a reputation for working well with that age group.

As the school year progressed, I noticed a distinct decline in my son's attitude toward school. At the beginning of the school year he looked forward to going to school. However, by December, he moped around and was short tempered toward anything having to do with school. I could see that David was beginning to withdraw and to shut everyone out of his life.

After several attempts to find out what was wrong, I finally went into his bedroom, sat down on his bed with him, and asked him what was wrong. He said he hated school. This was not like David. When I asked him why he no longer liked school, he said, "Because the teacher thinks I'm stupid." This startled me because of all the glowing things we had heard about the teacher, so I asked him why he believed she thought he was stupid. He answered, "Because she makes me sit in the dunce chair."

I contacted the teacher to find out what that meant. At first, she indicated she did not know what he meant by it. Upon careful examination of the situation I discovered what had happened. Sometime during the first week of school, she moved David from one part of the room to another for disciplinary reasons. However, she never moved him back. For three months he sat in the same chair, thinking he was being disciplined. Environmental factors had become a big issue with him in a way he could not understand. When I was willing to get into his world to talk about it with him, he was finally able to express his hurt in a way that helped me find out what was hurting him.

We need to be aware of environmental circumstances and body language when we are trying to communicate with each other. With a little attention to these details, we can enhance communication with one another immensely.

The Use of Feedback in Communication

A way to develop effective communication in any relationship is through feedback. Feedback is a technique by which we learn to listen to each other. Simply saying the message audibly does not mean that the one who hears the words will receive the message or that communication has taken place. Through feedback, the one receiving the message and the one sending the message work together to be sure that the message is clearly transmitted and received.

Chris and I began to develop the practice of feedback early in our marriage. When we sensed that we needed to do some serious communicating because of a misunderstanding between us, one of us would offer to be the receiver, and the other the transmitter. The one who was the designated transmitter in the feedback session was allowed to choose the topic of discussion. We would find a neutral location and a time when there would be as few interruptions as possible. We then would agree not to react to each other by raising our voices, disagreeing, going on the defense, using inflammatory words, or resorting to any of the other things that hinder communication. We limited the discussion to only one topic per feedback session.

When I volunteered to be the receiver and Chris was the transmitter, I would begin the session by asking, "Honey, if there was one thing that could be changed that would make you happy, what would it be?" Chris would then state her most pressing concern at the moment. Next, I would restate what she said in my own words, stating what I thought I heard. If that was not what Chris meant by her initial statement, she would then restate her message differently. Then, I would again restate what she said in my own words. This is what is meant by feedback.

We would continue the process of sending and receiving back and forth until we both agreed on the wording of the message and believed that we understood what the message was. In the early days, this may have taken three or four cycles of repeating the message in our own words until we fully understood what the other person was trying to say. The more proficient at feedback we became, the fewer times we had to restate the original message. The goal was to agree upon the issue of concern and to see it from each other's point of view. It is amazing how often, once we understood our partner's concern, the differences between us would disappear and a solution was quickly agreed upon.

As we continued to practice feedback in our marriage and as I was involved in marriage counseling, I detected an identifiable pattern of concern. I realized that this same pattern existed in the early years of my marriage as well. In those years, I often was concerned about my image as a successful husband, father, and pastor. Chris was concerned about such issues as financial security, the management of the home, and care of the children. I settled on two words, each one describing the general communication of a husband and a wife. For a husband, the word is *ego,* and for a wife, the word is *security.* For the husband, his general message is "feed my ego." For the wife, the general message is "meet my needs" (See diagram 3 on the next page).

My goal as a husband is to try to turn my basic message around to "I will meet your needs." My wife, on the other hand, seeks to turn her basic message around to "I will feed your ego" (See diagram 4 on page 83). Feedback will not work for individuals who are selfishly seeking to dominate each other. It only works when a couple genuinely desires to communicate effectively with each other and desires God's best for their marriage.

This same approach to communication works with other relationships as well. As our children reached the age when they could understand and participate, we included them in the feedback sessions when appropriate. It also works in churches. If the pastor of a

DIAGRAM 3

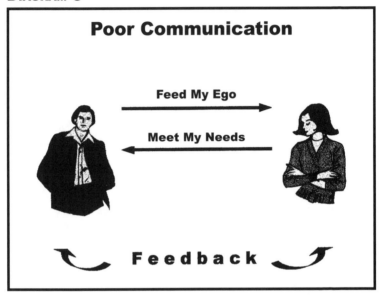

Poor Communication

Feed My Ego

Meet My Needs

F e e d b a c k

church can learn to communicate to his congregation "I will meet your needs," and the congregation communicates back to the pastor "We will meet your needs," good communication takes place. However, when the communication is negative, critical, and self-centered, the relationship is in deep trouble, whether it is husbands and wives, parents and children, pastors and churches, employers and employees.

Many times, what we say is meant to drive us apart rather than to unite us. By careless and faulty communication, we actually make matters worse. We must not wait until we are in a conflict or crisis situation to begin developing effective patterns of communication. They must be learned and in place well before conflicts arise. When parents and their children learn to communicate

DIAGRAM 4

Good Communication

I Will Meet Your Needs

I Will Feed Your Ego

Feedback

before the stress of adolescence, good communication can go a long way to lessening those stresses.

On one occasion, when my daughter was first beginning to date, she did something I considered to be a violation of her dating privileges. It was late at night when I confronted her in anger and then stomped off to bed. Before I got to the top of the stairs, I heard Tamara stamp her foot and say in a firm voice, "Dad, we have to talk this out now." She was relaying back to me a principle her mother and I sought to teach our children early, "BE ANGRY, AND YET DO NOT SIN; do not let the sun go down on your anger, and do not give the devil an opportunity" (Ephesians 4:26–27). She was right. I was wrong. What followed was a great time of communication and coming to a better understanding of the situation. I was thankful that we had taught her how to communicate before that night.

It is absolutely essential that we develop effective patterns of communication in any relationship and at every level, whether it is merely a relationship of circumstance or of purpose. No relationship will reach the level of fulfillment without effective communication. The good news is that anyone who sincerely desires to form healthy relationships can develop effective communication skills. Without effective communication, there can be no healthy relationships.

Avoid I-Am-Right-You-Are-Wrong Thinking

James instructed his readers, "[This] you know, my beloved brethren. But let everyone be quick to hear, slow to speak [and] slow to anger; for the anger of man does not achieve the righteousness of God" (James 1:19–20). The act of hearing in this verse does not refer simply to hearing audibly. It includes hearing with understanding. When we care more about what we are thinking than listening to others, there is little possibility of making any progress toward resolving conflicts.

Good communication requires both sending and receiving messages. We need to accept responsibility both for the messages we send and for the messages we receive. Because we do not want others to distort the message we send, we should not distort the message others send to us. Yet often we do distort the message by the way we think. Years ago, I heard a sermon with the theme "You are what you think even more than you think." More recently, I found the book *Telling Yourself the Truth* by William Backus and Marie Chapian to be very helpful in identifying and correcting my self-talk, and in counseling others regarding theirs.[3]

A major part of communication depends upon our thought life. Self-talk is the basis for all interpersonal relationships, including our communication with God. Many, if not all of us, spend too much time rehearsing negative thoughts in our minds, especially when we are in conflict situations. We think about how wrong the other person is and how right we are. Before long, we begin to minimize our own faults and maximize the faults of others. Gradually, there is a shift in our perceived reality. We do not recognize that we have crossed over the line from truth to falsehood. We become obsessed with our own perception and lose sight of what really matters. We become prisoners of our own minds. Those who study human behavior often refer to this process of thinking as *cognitive dissonance*.

Cognitive dissonance is a method of dealing with the tension between conflicting cognitive elements in our thinking. By cognitive elements I mean "any knowledge, opinion, or belief about the environment, about one's self, or about one's behavior."[4] Cognitive dissonance is:

> The mental conflict that occurs when beliefs or assumptions are contradicted by new information. The unease or tension that the conflict arouses in a person is relieved by one of several defensive maneuvers: the person rejects, explains away, or avoids the new

information, persuades himself that no conflict really exists, reconciles the difference, or resorts to any other defensive means of preserving stability or order in his conception of the world and of himself.[5]

In other words, our faulty thought processes take over and we are no longer able to receive correctly the other person's message. When we resort to cognitive dissonance as a way of dealing with the difficult problems in our lives, we actually make recovering from those problems more difficult, and we prolong the healing process. We do not have to become budding psychologists in order to observe when someone else is resorting to cognitive dissonance. The difficulty is recognizing when we are doing it ourselves.

There are many tools in the arsenal of cognitive dissonance that form parts of our faulty thinking. We minimize our faults and maximize the faults of others. We expand the importance of our views and trivialize the views of others. We project blame onto others when we are the ones to blame. We deny the truth of others and the falsehood of our own views. It has been said that many individuals on death row who are genuinely guilty of murder have come to believe they are not guilty, because they have rehearsed the matter over and over again, year after year, until they themselves believe the big lie. Cognitive dissonance turns truth into lies and lies into truth.

God, speaking through Jeremiah the prophet, described the conditions in Jeremiah's day:

"And they bend their tongue [like] their bow; lies and not truth prevail in the land; For they proceed from evil to evil, and they do not know me," declares the LORD. "Let everyone be on guard against his neighbor, and do not trust any brother; because every brother deals craftily, and every neighbor goes about as a slanderer. And everyone deceives his neighbor and does not speak the truth, They have taught their tongue to speak lies; They weary themselves committing iniquity. Your dwelling is in the midst of deceit; through deceit they refuse to know me," declares the LORD." (Jeremiah 9:3–6)

We live in a society that is becoming more and more polarized every day because of cognitive dissonance. Politicians running for office are masters at creating cognitive dissonance in order to win elections. They build up their own worth while tearing down their opponents. The media finds they can captivate the public by enhancing their story line with cognitive dissonance. Talk shows on television and radio peddle cognitive dissonance to gain an audience. They often pit opposing views against each other and belittle one view while embellishing the other. In the same way, the entertainment and advertising industries thrive on cognitive dissonance.

The concept of cognitive dissonance has even been touted as a method of helping young people learn in school. Studies have been conducted by educational psychologists whereby students are confronted with conflicting cognitive elements. Then, an attempt is made to measure the amount of cognitive dissonance created by those conflicting elements to see how much dissonance is displayed. A little cognitive dissonance can promote a healthy introspection of the student's beliefs. However, it also can very easily undermine some of the fundamental values parents want to instill in their child.

As a parent, I was always watchful of what my children were learning in school. When a teacher attempted to stir up one of my children through cognitive dissonance, I was there to confront that teacher. Stirring up turmoil in the minds of the students under the guise of teaching them to think for themselves can very easily become a way of manipulating the child and causing the child to question basic beliefs of the child and his or her family.

One example in our family occurred when our son was attending a junior high school civics class. The teacher held the political view that the Vietnam War was an immoral war and expressed this frequently to the class. When David said he did not believe this, the teacher gave him an assignment in which he was required to debate the issue against his stated view. Had this been a class on debate or forensics in high school, this would have been an appropriate assignment. However, it appeared to David and to me that the teacher was merely seeking to humiliate him in front of his classmates because he disagreed with her. She was trying to create cognitive dissonance in him so he would change his views. I waited for a period of time to see if David could handle the situation without my intervention. When he indicated to me that he could not, I confronted the teacher and she backed down. Creating cognitive dissonance was clearly not a proper method of teaching in that situation.

Holding a firm conviction regarding matters of this life is not the same as resorting to cognitive dissonance. We need to teach and model correct thinking to our children. Leon Festinger, the first to formulate cognitive dissonance theory, presented an interesting observation about human behavior when he wrote:

> A man with a conviction is a hard man to change. Tell him you disagree and he turns away. Show him facts or figures and he questions your sources. Appeal to logic and he fails to see your point.
>
> We have all experienced the futility of trying to change a strong conviction, especially if the convinced person has some investment in the belief. We are familiar with the variety of ingenious defenses with which people protect their convictions, managing to keep them unscathed through the most devastating attacks.
>
> But man's resourcefulness goes beyond simply protecting a belief. Suppose an individual believes something with his whole heart; suppose that he has a commitment to his belief, that he has taken irrevocable actions because of it. Finally, suppose that he is presented with evidence, unequivocal and undeniable evidence, that the belief is wrong. What will happen? The individual will frequently emerge, not only unshaken but more convinced of the truth of the belief than ever before. Indeed, he may even show

a new fervor about convincing and converting other people to his view.[6]

Festinger was writing about a religious person. Both Christians and non-Christians engage in cognitive dissonance thinking. It has become a way of life inside and outside the church. Many times, we resort to this kind of thinking in order to win arguments, get our way, or win elections. When adults—parents, teachers, politicians, and religious leaders—resort to this kind of thinking, is it any wonder that our children learn it also? As was stated earlier, children do not mirror the mistakes of adults; they magnify them. One of the tools we teach them to use as a magnifying glass is cognitive dissonance.

If we are ever going to find answers to the problems of society, we are going to have to look at our own thought processes and inner reasoning. Are we telling ourselves the truth, or are we resorting to cognitive dissonance? When we dialogue with others who disagree with us, do we embellish our point of view and depreciate theirs? Do we blame others and fail to acknowledge our own weaknesses?

Jesus instructed His disciples:

> And why do you look at the speck that is in your brother's eye, but do not notice the log that is in your own eye? Or how can you say to your brother, "Let me take the speck out of your eye," and behold, the log is in your own eye? You hypocrite, first take the log out of your own eye, and then you will

see clearly to take the speck out of your brother's eye. (Mathew 7:3–5)

The speck in our own eye is held there by cognitive dissonance. Cognitive dissonance begins with faulty communication with self. Then it spills over into our communication with others. It is perhaps one of the greatest hindrances to healthy communication and prevents us from achieving healthy relationships. We need to learn the art of communicating truth, an art that has almost been lost. Instead of shouting across the chasms that divide us, we must learn to communicate with each other by saying only what is true and no more.

For years there has been a chasm referred to as "the generation gap." However, it is no longer a gap between generations; it is a gap between adults, between youth, between husbands and wives, between parents and their children, between races, between ethnic groups, between political parties, and between church members. It exists in every city, in small towns, and in rural areas. It seems like we all have agendas and that we become so zealous for our own point of view that we fail to achieve the basic necessities for any society to exist: healthy relationships and good communication.

Like everyone else, I had painful experiences in life that distorted my view of reality. I developed the bad habit of resorting to cognitive dissonance in dealing with those hurts. However, it was not until I was willing to change my own self-talk that true healing in my life began. I needed to stop blaming my adopted parents for my problems. Yes, they were the cause of many of my problems, but not all of them. They taught me many good things, sometimes in spite of themselves. They were not all bad, and I surely was not all good. The older I get, the more I need to accept responsibility for my own behavior and stop blaming others in my past. Maybe if we adults start telling each other the truth without engaging in cognitive dissonance thinking, we will be able to help the next generation find a way out of the troubles they are facing.

If the truth is negative, we need to say it is negative. However, there is a pattern of thinking that has slipped into the American psychic almost without notice. I first noticed it in a family member who frequently ended a statement with ". . . and I'm not the only one who feels this way." This habit was so noticeable that my wife and I began to listen to each other to see if we also had the habit. We were surprised at the number of times we ended our statements in the same way.

I began searching for the source of the phenomenon and found that it probably came from the nightly news on television. Almost every news item is bolstered by, ". . . and he is not the only one who thinks this way." In our family, we call it *awfullizing*. We tend to stretch the truth a little in order to make the subject matter weightier. If we are not careful, our conversation becomes steeped in negative thinking. When that happens, we tend to pull each other down by our conversation instead of lifting each other up. Young people seem to detect this type of thinking before adults do and are turned off by it.

Paul wrote:

> Finally, brethren, whatever is true, whatever is honorable, whatever is right, whatever is pure, whatever is lovely, whatever is of good repute, if there is any excellence and if anything worthy of praise, let your mind dwell on these things. (Philippians 4:8)

In another place, he wrote: "Let your speech always be with grace, seasoned, as it were, with salt, so that you may know how you should respond to each person" (Colossians 4:6).

Before we can talk about philosophies or ever hope to change the philosophies that are harmful, we need to recognize the importance of relationships and communication to the process of change. The title of this book is *Can We Talk?* We may never reach agreement on questions regarding when the universe came into being or about heaven and hell and things to come. We may not even agree as to how important these matters are. Yet by acknowledging that we still are related to each other and that this relationship is worthwhile, we have taken the first step toward solving problems having to do with matters of this life. When we learn to communicate the truth about matters of this life, then we have taken a second step toward resolving conflicts in society, in our churches, and in our families.

One of the reasons we do not see ourselves as interrelated and do not communicate well with each other is because too often we believe it is more profitable to emphasize our differences. In fact, there are many organizations that exist solely to exploit differences for the personal gain of the members of the organization. They see disagreement more profitable than agreement and, therefore, expend a lot of resources to foster disagreement. When Christians act as if it is more profitable to disagree than to agree, we are no better than any other organization that seeks to maintain disagreements rather than work together to resolve conflicts.

In order to find out why we refuse to see ourselves as interrelated and refuse to expend the effort to communicate, we need to examine some of our basic philosophies; specifically, our philosophies regarding knowledge, existence, and behavior. Every other philosophy falls under these three categories. It is through these philosophies that we deny our interrelatedness, and it is in defense of these philosophies that we error most in communicating with each other.

PART II

PHILOSOPHIES THAT
DESTROY RELATIONSHIPS

CHAPTER THREE

How We View Knowledge
Divides Us

When tragedies overtake us, the first word that often comes to mind is *why*? This is especially true when the tragedy is of human origin, as in the case of the Littleton shooting. There is no limit to the number of answers given, each from a different point of view. However, in order to sort out the correct answer, we have to be able to understand what we are saying. Even when we use the same words, we may not be saying the same thing. Words must have a context in order to have meaning. By learning to understand the context of other people, we learn to communicate in ways they can understand and to receive their messages consistently.

One of the first contexts to understand, and one most often overlooked, is our perspective of life itself. By this, I mean our philosophy of life. An interesting result of many tragedies where lives have been disrupted is how radically different one's perspective of life is following the tragedy, particularly when there is a great loss of life and personal property.

This book is not meant to be a philosophical treatise, and so what is presented here is very concise. Yet I believe that a simple presentation of these basic philosophies of life will assist us in our dialogue as we seek to answer the question *Why?*

There are basically three categories of philosophy that govern our lives: our philosophy about knowledge, our philosophy about existence, and our philosophy about behavior. These are three perspectives from which we view life. We all hold some views in each of these areas, even though we may not be able to explain them at any given moment in time. Still, they govern our lives. These philosophies may exist simultaneously and may even contradict each other. Jim Leffel, in an article on postmodernism, wrote:

> Affirmative postmodernists are more difficult to describe because they are active in so many diverse causes. Indeed, eclecticism (borrowing from a variety of worldviews) and an ability to maintain even contradictory positions simultaneously are common among affirmative postmodernists. They argue that self-contradiction isn't a problem once we remove the modernist burden of rational consistency.[1]

Postmodernists are not the first to hold contradictory ideas. Such contradictions have been around for a long time. In this section on philosophies that divide us, we will see that these three broad areas of philosophy are often very contradictory. The ability to live by contradictory philosophies is primarily the fruit of cognitive dissonance thinking.

Through cognitive dissonance we become masters at defending our philosophies in spite of the contradictions. Having divergent philosophies alone is not what causes division between us. It is how we use these philosophies against each other that causes problems. For every perceived conflict between us, there is a ready-made philosophy by which we justify continuing the conflict. The way we use these conflicting philosophies is like children playing games.

THE GAME: "I KNOW SOMETHING YOU DON'T KNOW"

"I know something you don't know" is a common playground taunt of children. What really makes the person being teased angry is when that is followed by, "And I'm not going to tell you." The next step in the game is, "You are not smart enough to understand." To reinforce the effects of this game, children often create new words or give old words new meanings.

In the Littleton incident, it was reported that the "in crowd" taunted members of the Trench Coat Mafia. In return, the response of those being taunted was to talk back in German. It is obvious that the purpose was not to communicate in a language familiar to both sides but to use language to further separate them. This is not to excuse the "in crowd." The point is that communication broke down on both sides. The most obvious indicators of this breakdown were on the part of the group perceived as outcasts. They developed both verbal and nonverbal ways of sending messages that were not understandable and were meant to further divide.

Rules of the Game

"I know something you don't know" is painful for those who are being discriminated against. I experienced it as a young person, both at school and at home. In grade school, I began to notice that others treated me as if I was different. I was usually the youngest and biggest in the class. Taunts of "dummy" were hurled at me on the playground. This carried over into the classroom. We give this game special names today. We call it "learning disabilities," "fetal alcohol syndrome," and other high-sounding names. I do not mean to imply there are not some identifiable problems with learning in some children. However, research has shown that many children classified as having learning disabilities are often some of the brightest. The problem is that they do not learn the same way others do or the way the school system requires them to learn. Labeling those children can be very detrimental to helping them overcome their problems and, when the labels stick, can isolate the child even more from those with whom they need healthy relationships.

One day, when I was in junior high, my class was invited to join the high school in a college-prep assembly. The teacher asked all of the students who planned to attend college to raise their hands. They would be given the privilege of attending the assembly. I raised my hand along with the rest of the class. As I was leaving the classroom, the teacher took me aside and asked, "You're not going to college, are you?" By this question she confirmed what I was sure everyone believed about me—that I was dumb.

This game was played at home on the farm as well. As I worked in the fields alongside the hired men and other family members, they teased me by calling me "Slow Moe." The memory of those taunts is still very painful today. I can appreciate how others feel when they receive this sort of treatment.

After I was discharged from the Navy, I returned to the family farm. I still believed that the problems from earlier years in the family were primarily my fault. I endeavored to try harder. Yet the taunts continued. Finally, I decided that my only recourse was to go to college. It was then that I realized the seriousness of the game. When I announced my intentions, my adopted parents told me I was not smart enough to go to college. I literally ran away from home one last time.

Where do young people learn the game of "I know something you don't know"? They learn it from adults. Throughout human history, mankind has used knowledge, or the withholding of knowledge, to divide. It is a small step between believing that someone else *does* not know to believing that they *cannot* know. When that circle of logic—or rather illogic—is complete, it is called *Gnosticism*. The word comes from the Greek word *gnosis*, meaning "to know."

In general, Gnosticism is the belief that some people are better than others because of what they know. I use *Gnosticism* to refer to any knowledge that man claims to have learned on his own, apart from God. In Gnosticism, knowing certain things is the path to salvation. Throughout history, this kind of knowledge was called mysteries. When the Bible talks about mysteries, it is always referring to a truth that was formerly hidden but has now been revealed by God (Ephesians 3:4–7). When men use the term, it often means something unknowable, hidden, or secret.

Belonging to secret organizations that have mysterious rituals has intrigued mankind since the Garden of Eden. My adopted parents were members of several organizations that used passwords and engaged in secret rituals. One particular organization met every month. As a child, I was taken to the meetings and was left to sit in the women's lounge until the secret portion of the meeting was over. I was never allowed to see what went on in those meetings but could hear sounds that seemed strange because of the secrecy. They probably were no more mysterious than individuals marching across a hardwood floor in a cavernous room, but to a child the sounds were foreboding.

Each Gnostic sect uses their own set of rituals to heighten the mysteries they claim to possess. The mysteries may be earthy or supernatural knowledge. The salvation they claim to provide may be freedom from poverty, freedom from physical ailments, or psychological and emotional freedom. Some claim to be able to solve all of life's problems or society's ills through their superior knowledge.

Because that knowledge is acquired through human means, it is subjective knowledge. Subjective knowledge—knowledge without objective verification—can be very divisive because the one who thinks he holds the key to that knowledge sets himself up to judge others who don't have it. Historically, Gnosticism has covered the full spectrum of human philosophies but most often has been viewed in contradistinction to any objective supernatural knowledge or revelation. With the rise of naturalism and humanism, mystical knowledge has been out of vogue. However, the tide away from mystical knowledge is turning. There are more and more individuals and groups claiming some special power to receive mysterious truth from some hidden force in the universe.

The origin of Gnosticism can be traced back to the time of the first-century church. It can also be found in both Jewish and Greek philosophy before Christ. It might have been part of what the Bible refers to as the confusion of languages in the account of the tower of Babel in Genesis 11. Moses recorded God's words, "Come, let Us go down and there confuse their language, that they may not understand one another's speech" (Genesis 11:7). That judgment came because the people sought to find their own way into heaven apart from the one true God of the universe.

Gnosticism probably even goes back to the Fall in the Garden of Eden, when Satan put a spin on God's words and questioned, "Has God said? . . ." (Genesis 3:1). We cannot put all the blame on Satan, because Eve also put her spin on God's words when she misquoted Him. She even put words into God's mouth when she told Satan God had forbidden them to touch the fruit (Genesis 3:3).

In our relationships and communication with each other, we have a tendency to garble the message by adding our own meaning to words. The next step is to create an apparent chasm between us by deciding that, since the other person does not understand our encoded message, they are not as smart as we are or as good as we are. We might even carry it further and decide that they are not as important as we are, or not important at all, so we can dismiss or even eliminate them.

The process of dividing into Gnostic groups may start innocently enough as a silly prank, but soon it snowballs into an avalanche of hatred and recrimination. Historically, the Christian church has been as guilty of Gnosticism as the rest of the world. Toward the end of the first century, roots of this harmful philosophy crept into the church. John wrote his Gospel and his three epistles to counteract this philosophy. This is why his Gospel account of Jesus, written perhaps as late as A.D. 90 is so different from the three synoptic Gospels— Matthew, Mark, and Luke. They wrote their Gospels approximately thirty years before John wrote his. In John's day, many taught that to be saved one needed to be initiated into some mysterious truth, a truth that only a few were able to understand.

While there were many forms of Gnosticism in John's day, one of the early commonalities among different

Gnostic sects was that there were two parts to the universe: matter and spirit. It was taught that matter was evil and spirit was good. To them, salvation was the ability to move from the material world into the spiritual world through some mysterious truth available only to a few. This was accomplished through knowledge (gnosis). By extension, they taught that not everyone was able to move from the material world to the spiritual world, because not everyone was able to understand these mysteries.

Winners and Losers

As this philosophy developed, mankind was divided into three groups: the pneumatics, the psychics, and the hylics. Concerning this division, Alexander Renwick wrote:

> The Gnostic claimed special esoteric or secret knowledge. It could be possessed only by that section of humanity which was "pneumatic," or spiritual. They alone were inevitably led back to the realm of light of the Supreme God. There was a second class of men, those who were only "psychic" and could not get beyond faith. The prophets and other good Hebrews belonged to this class but they must be eternally in the sphere much inferior to that occupied by those who had "gnosis." A third class represented the overwhelming mass of human kind. They were merely "hylic" (i.e., subject to matter) and their case was utterly hopeless for they were in endless bondage to Satan and their own lusts, and their end was

to be completely destroyed. Here was one of the worst features of Gnosticism, the elevating of a limited number into a specially privileged class, and the consigning of the vast majority of mankind to unredeemable destruction.[2]

Gnosticism took two opposite directions in its application to everyday life. Since they held the view that physical life was evil, one application was to deny the needs of the physical body. This is known as *asceticism*. The other direction was that, since the physical life was not a part of the higher spiritual existence, what was done in the physical life was of no consequence. This led to the practice of licentiousness, or the freedom to indulge the physical body at will.

By the second century, the philosophy of Gnosticism took on added meaning as it was applied to the way the Bible was interpreted. A man by the name of Origen (A.D. 185–254) devised a method of interpreting the Bible called the *allegorical method*. In his method, he saw three levels of meaning: the literal, the moral, and the spiritual. Thus, there were multiple meanings in the Bible. What the interpreter saw in the text was more important than what the author meant by what was written. It led to a very subjective approach to interpreting the Bible called allegorical interpretation.

Paul Tan, in his book *The Interpretation of Prophecy*, gives an excellent description of this approach to interpretation:

> In early church history, there arose a group of interpreters (known as the "allegorists") which saw a

multiplicity of senses and meanings in the Scriptures. They regarded the literal words only as a vehicle for arriving at the hidden, more spiritual, and more profound sense of Scripture. "What was more natural, more in keeping with all of creation," reasoned the allegorists, "than that God should have concealed a spiritual message in crude material language. . . . Interpretation, therefore, lay in discerning the spiritual meaning of the text hidden beneath the letter, which could often for all practical purposes be discarded."[3]

The allegorists not only affirmed the concept of multiple sense in Scripture but also decreed that the hidden, deeper sense was the *real* one. The Alexandrians and other church fathers practiced allegorism to the hilt, and the fanciful exegeses they produced "make one part of our mind laugh and another part groan."[4]

Allegorization was a handy tool for the Gnostics to promote their mysteries in the early church. To them, what the author of the Bible meant was not as important as the mysterious truths they found through this subjective approach. Allegorical interpretation continues to be popular in many branches of Christendom today. This Gnostic aberration was a major factor that led the church and the world into what historians call the Dark Ages. For centuries, church leaders used this method of interpreting Scripture to elevate themselves above the commoners and to subjugate the masses.

Over twenty-five years ago, when I first began to study Gnosticism and tried alerting others to its dangers, I was usually met with scorn or, at the very least, raised eyebrows. Who would ever believe that? I no longer receive those responses. While Gnosticism as a broad-based philosophy never died out, the name fell into disuse and was replaced with various other titles.

This widely divergent philosophy is everywhere today. Any group or sect that believes that their knowledge is mysterious or unknowable to others, or that salvation is through knowledge, is practicing Gnosticism. It is prevalent in much of what is called the New Age movement. Many forms of atheistic humanism are branches of the early false philosophy called Gnosticism but without the concept of God. In effect, humanism sees man as the ultimate source of knowledge. Hence, I place this belief system under the head of Gnosticism because it is knowledge apart from God's special revelation. A recent search of the term on the Internet demonstrated that many sects are once again openly identifying themselves as Gnostics.

The most poignant example of Gnosticism that comes to mind is the Heaven's Gate cult that captured the attention of the world a few years ago. Thirty-nine individuals in a mass-suicide pact took their own lives as the comet Hale-Bopp passed the earth. Among the many strange beliefs of the group, was the belief that they were about to move from the realm of earth to a higher level of being. They believed that there are two levels of existence on earth, one higher than the other. A third level could only be experienced when they shed their earthly bodies. The method by which they believed they moved from a lower level to a higher level was through knowledge that only they could comprehend.

One of the startling discoveries at the scene of the suicide was that many of the men had been castrated. This ominous aspect of this group ties back to Origen. Origen practiced a severe form of asceticism, including having himself emasculated in order to live what to him was a more pious lifestyle.[5]

Many young people have become involved in Gnostic groups through various means. Much of the influence is subtle and probably harmless. Yet because of the prevalence of mind control through cognitive dissonance in many of those groups, there is a point at which a line is crossed. In its extreme form, Gnosticism is very dangerous. In its milder form it creates havoc in society because of its tendency to separate groups of people and to prevent meaningful dialogue necessary to overcome conflicts among these groups.

REFUSING TO PLAY THE GAME: "I KNOW SOMETHING YOU DON'T KNOW"

One way the Christian community can help, such as in the dialogue concerning the Littleton tragedy, is to clearly delineate between the gospel message and the false teaching of salvation through knowledge or Gnosticism. The Christian gospel teaches that salvation comes through a personal relationship with the self-revealing God, who desires a relationship with mankind. John wrote, "In Him was life, and the life was the light of men" (John 1:4). Paul warned the church at Corinth regarding the practice of Gnosticism, ". . . knowledge makes arrogant, but love edifies" (1 Corinthians 8:1). To the church at Colossae, he wrote:

> Therefore let no one act as your judge in regard to food or drink or in respect to a festival or a new moon or a Sabbath day—things which are a [mere] shadow of what is to come; but the substance belongs to Christ. Let no one keep defrauding you of your prize by delighting in self-abasement and the worship of the angels, taking his stand on [visions] he has seen, *inflated without cause by his fleshly mind,* and not holding fast to the head, from whom the entire body, being supplied and held together by the joints and ligaments, grows with a growth which is from God. If you have died with Christ to the elementary principles of the world, why, as if you were living in the world, do you submit yourself to decrees, such as, "Do not handle, do not taste, do not touch!" (which all [refer] [to] things destined to perish with the using)—in accordance with the commandments and teachings of men? *These are matters which have, to be sure, the appearance of wisdom in self-made religion and self-abasement and severe treatment of the body, [but are] of no value against fleshly indulgence.* (Colossians 2:16–23, italics mine)

John, in his Gospel, was very careful to separate salvation through a personal relationship with Jesus Christ from the false teaching that salvation comes through knowing something esoteric. He didn't change the gospel message from that of the synoptic gospels but sought to purge the evil and divisive philosophies that many added to the gospel.

In order to counteract the false dichotomy of *dualism*, in which the material world is evil and the spirit world is good, John emphasized the physical body of Jesus. The first miracle Jesus performed was the changing of water into wine at the marriage feast in Cana (John 2:1–11). Thus, Jesus put His stamp of approval on the material element of wine and the physical relationship of marriage. This is not to say that Christians should engage in the use of alcoholic beverages. There are very good reasons for abstaining from drinking alcohol, especially because of the abuse of alcohol in America. What Jesus taught by this miracle was that wine is not inherently evil, as in the teaching of dualism.

Another way John counteracted the teaching of Gnosticism was to avoid the use of abstract concepts, such as faith and wisdom, which in his day carried Gnostic connotations. For example, the words *knowledge* (gnosis) and faith are not found in his Gospel. John avoided referring to abstract concepts because the Gnostics gave their own twisted meaning to these concepts and used them to elevate themselves above others. The gospel is not meant to exclude anyone on the basis of his or her inability to know some abstract truth. Those who teach this are teaching a false gospel.

The Greek term *gnosis* occurs only twice in the four Gospels, both in Luke's Gospel. The first time is in conjunction with the prophecy concerning John the Baptist. John the Baptist's father, Zacharias, praised God for the birth of his son saying, "And you, child, will be called the prophet of the Most High; For you will go on BEFORE THE LORD TO PREPARE HIS WAYS; To give to His people

[the] *knowledge* of salvation by the forgiveness of their sins" (Luke 1:76–77, italics mine). God used John the Baptist to introduce Jesus as the Savior of the world. Salvation through Jesus Christ is not through knowledge as an abstract idea or mysterious knowledge. It is salvation through a personal relationship with Jesus as Savior, which is obtained by being born of God. This was the knowledge the Baptist presented.

KNOWLEDGE VERSUS KNOWING

The second and last time the Greek term *gnosis* is used in the Gospels is Luke 11:52, where Jesus says, "Woe to you lawyers! For you have taken away the key of knowledge; you did not enter in yourselves, and those who were entering in you hindered" (Luke 11:52). These lawyers were also called scribes. They were men schooled in the Old Testament who used their subjective interpretation of the Old Testament to elevate themselves above the people, forcing the people to come to them instead of leading them to God. They actually prevented others from coming to a personal knowledge of God (Matthew 23:13). By setting themselves up as the final arbiter of truth, they denied the existence of objective absolute truth.

Wherever there is a denial of absolute truth, Gnosticism is present. A denial of absolute truth is warp and woof of the overall process of rejecting God and any responsibility to Him. Paul wrote:

> For the wrath of God is revealed from heaven against all ungodliness and unrighteousness of men,

111

who suppress the truth in unrighteousness, because that which is known about God is evident within them; for God made it evident to them. For since the creation of the world His invisible attributes, His eternal power and divine nature, have been clearly seen, being understood through what has been made, so that they are without excuse. (Romans 1:18–20)

One important noun John uses over and over in his Gospel is *truth*. John wrote:

And the Word became flesh, and dwelt among us, and we beheld His glory, glory as of the only begotten from the Father, full of grace and truth. (John 1:14)

For the Law was given through Moses; grace and truth were realized through Jesus Christ. (John 1:17)

Jesus therefore was saying to those Jews who had believed Him, "If you abide in My word, [then] you are truly disciples of Mine; and you will know the truth, and the truth shall make you free." (John 8:31–32)

Jesus said to him, "I am the way, and the truth, and the life; no one comes to the Father but through Me. (John 14:6)

But when He, the Spirit of truth, comes, He will guide you into all the truth; for He will not speak on His own initiative, but whatever He hears, He will speak; and He will disclose to you what is to come. (John 16:13)

We can see that truth regarding salvation is not abstract; it is concrete and knowable. It is found through having a personal relationship with Jesus Christ as revealed by God in the Bible. When a person comes into a personal relationship with Christ after being born of God, God gives that person the Holy Spirit to enable him or her to understand the truth. Men can know a lot of facts about the universe around them but not know the truth about those facts.

In our day, Gnostics tell us that all truth is relative. In this way, they avoid submitting to the truth. Through high-sounding rationality, they put themselves above truth and become judges of truth. Like the lawyers of Jesus' day, Gnostics are robbing this generation of the knowledge of the truth.

By declaring all truth relative and placing themselves above it, modern-day Gnostics place their opinions above everyone else's, including God's opinion. Truth is then manipulated to their advantage. Morality is determined by the situation. This is called *situational ethics*. The term *Gnostic* still applies because the situational ethicist manipulates knowledge in much the same way that ancient Gnostics did. Yet, even today, Gnosticism continues to evolve at a breakneck speed. About the time we begin to understand their methods and reasoning, they change.

For the past several decades, American culture has been conforming to what some have termed modernism. In an attempt to deny any semblance of objective truth, modernists teach:

Humans are purely material machines. We live in a purely physical world. Nothing exists beyond what our senses perceive. Humans are self-governing and free to choose their own direction. People should be "rationalistic optimists" who depend only on the data of their senses and reason.[6]

The crowning achievement of modernism, with its emphasis upon self-government and individual freedom, is the U.S. Constitution and a government of the people, by the people, and for the people. The pendulum is now swinging in the opposite direction from modernism to postmodernism. Postmodernism suits the concepts of globalism and one-world government. In postmodernism:

Humans are cogs in a social machine. We are primarily social beings. People are the product of their culture and only imagine they are self-governing. There is no such thing as objective rationality (that is, reason unaffected by bias) in the sense that modernists use the term. Objective reason is a myth.[7]

A clear understanding of God's revelation refutes postmodernism. The Bible is very specific in its teaching regarding knowing the truth. There are two terms translated "to know" in the Greek New Testament. The first is *ginosko* (the verb form of *gnosis*) and the second is *oida*. As with any word in the New Testament, the meaning of these two terms must be learned from the contexts in which they are found. For our purpose, we need to see that *ginosko* suggests "coming to know, knowing by experience," and hence a relationship between the one who knows and what is known. On the other hand, *oida* suggests "perception" and hence knowledge acquired with or without any personal relationship with the object known. *Ginosko* would correspond closely with what we call subjective knowledge. *Oida* would correspond to objective knowledge and is the term used when referring to divine revelation.[8]

Instead of seeing humans as purely material machines as the modernist does, or as cogs in a social machine as the postmodernist does, God declares that He is the ultimate source of truth. Any knowledge that we possess that is consistent with His truth has been made known to us by His will through divine revelation. This truth exists apart from us as human beings, and we are given the opportunity to experience this truth through our relationship with God through Christ. The salvation of the Bible comes through our relationship with God, who is ultimate truth, and not through knowledge that can be manipulated by men. Therefore, both our perception of truth (oida) and our relationship to truth (ginosko) come from God. What is important is not how much knowledge we have but the validity of the knowledge. This is good news! It insures that salvation is available to anyone who will receive His Son, Jesus Christ. John wrote:

> And the witness is this, that God has given us eternal life, and this life is in His Son. He who has the Son has the life; he who does not have the Son of God does not have the life. (1 John 5:11–12)

We can see that eternal life comes through a personal relationship with Christ and not through knowledge. Since this is true, what role does the act of believing play in salvation? To answer this, it is important to notice how John distinguished between individuals who believe something momentarily and those who demonstrate a permanent change in their character. In other words, their character reflects what they believe.

Early in Jesus' ministry, in John 2:23, John noted, "Now when He was in Jerusalem at the Passover, during the feast, many believed in His name, observing His signs which He was doing." The verb tense used here suggests action at a moment in time without reference to beginning or end. Greek grammarians call it *point* or *punctiliar* action.[9] John clarified this kind of believing with the following statement, "But Jesus, on His part, was not entrusting Himself to them, for He knew all men, and because He did not need anyone to bear witness concerning man for He Himself knew what was in man" (John 2:24–25). These individuals who believed were not necessarily saved because they believed. In fact, this dilemma is presented and answered by John's Gospel. The question is, how is it possible that some believed but did not possess eternal life? The answer is, they were not born from above.

The type of believing in John 2:23 is in contrast to the type of believing mentioned in the prologue of the Gospel. In chapter 1, verse 12, John wrote, "But as many as received Him, to them He gave the right to become children of God, [even] to those who believe in His name." Here the type of believing implies an attendant change in character consistent with what is believed. The grammatical construction in the original language that describes this change of character is called a *present active participle*.[10] It is a verbal idea used as an adjective that describes the character of the individual.

John consistently uses the present active participle in his Gospel and, for the most part, reserves the present active participle to refer to individuals whose actions reflect their inner character. Some of these verbal ideas are *believing, receiving, following, hearing, abiding,* and *living*. In instances where these verbal adjectives are used, they could accurately be translated as *believers, receivers, followers, hearers, abiders,* and *livers*.

A good example of the importance of this grammatical construct is that of a runner. If I observed a man running down the street, I might think he is a runner. However, if someone else who knew the man saw him running, he would know the man was not a runner but was merely in a hurry at that moment in time.

John was very careful to tell us that the change from believing momentarily to being a believer does not come simply because someone knows something. He stated categorically regarding Jesus' teaching, "What He has seen and heard, of that He bears witness; and no man receives His witness" (John 3:32). In other words, no human being, in and of himself, is able to receive the gospel message. No one is saved simply by believing. Salvation does not come through knowledge. The ability to believe unto eternal life is the result of being born again.

John's full statement reads:

What He has seen and heard, of that He bears witness; and no man receives His witness. He who has received [present active participle] His witness has set his seal to [this], that God is true. For He whom God has sent speaks the words of God; for He gives the Spirit without measure. The Father loves the Son, and has given all things into His hand. He who believes in the Son has eternal life; but he who does not obey the Son shall not see life, but the wrath of God abides on him. (John 3:32–36, italics mine)

The statement "he who has received" could correctly be translated into English as "the receiver." The statement "he who believes" can correctly be translated "the believer." This correctly renders the verbal idea, which in the Greek describes the character of the subject of the sentence. John made it clear that it is not some innate ability to receive the message that makes a person a child of God; it is the power of the Holy Spirit working in the life of the person who has a relationship with God through Jesus Christ.

This takes us back to the previous context in John 3, where Nicodemus, a very knowledgeable Jewish teacher, still needed to be born again. Jesus tells him, "Truly, truly, I say to you, unless one is born again he cannot see the kingdom of God" (John 3:3). This was confusing to Nicodemus because he had been taught from childhood that knowing the Old Testament was all he needed in order to be a part of God's kingdom. In fact, Jesus goes on to say that being born again is the work of the Holy Spirit, and no man can fully understand how the Holy Spirit works. Jesus said:

> Do not marvel that I said to you, "You must be born again." The wind blows where it wishes and you hear the sound of it, but do not know where it comes from and where it is going; so is everyone who is born of the Spirit. (John 3:7–8)

Later in the chapter, John wrote, "He who believes in the Son has eternal life" (John 3:36). Here we have another present active participle. It could correctly be rendered into English as "the believer in the Son has eternal life." This is not a statement regarding how one obtains eternal life but a statement of fact regarding a believer. Jesus, Himself, told us how a person receives eternal life. He taught, "My sheep hear My voice, and I know them, and they follow Me; and *I give eternal life to them*, and they shall never perish; and no one shall snatch them out of My hand" (John 10:27–28, italics mine). Eternal life is a gift given by the Savior.

Salvation is not acquired through some esoteric knowledge or even by believing the truth. The ability to believe is the result of salvation, not the means of salvation. Because Gnosticism continues to mutate, Christians are going to need to know the difference in order to know the truth. There is no power to save in the Gnostic gospel, though many still believe in it and think they are saved.

Someone might object, "But doesn't Paul say we have to believe in order to be saved?" Yes, he does. In Romans

10:9, Paul wrote, ". . . if you confess with your mouth Jesus [as] Lord, and believe in your heart that God raised Him from the dead, you will be saved." Notice the context. Paul was talking about the Jews who had knowledge—the knowledge revealed to them through God's prophets—and still they were not saved. He wrote:

> Brethren, my heart's desire and my prayer to God for them is for [their] salvation. For I testify about them that they have a zeal for God, but not in accordance with knowledge. For not knowing about God's righteousness and seeking to establish their own, they did not subject themselves to the righteousness of God. For Christ is the end of the law for righteousness to everyone who believes. (Romans 10:1–4)

The problem was that they chose to replace the righteousness that comes through faith with a righteousness they achieved by their own works. They knew the truth but rejected it demonstrating they were not believers. Paul wrote, "For by grace you have been saved through faith; and that not of yourselves, [it is] the gift of God; not as a result of works, that no one may boast" (Ephesians 2:8–9). Salvation is a free gift; this is what *grace* means. Faith is the channel through which we appropriate this gift. Faith is also part of this gift. It is totally illogical to assume that God would give us a gift and then not also give us the ability to receive it. On the other hand, it is equally illogical to assume that those who do not have eternal life are not saved because they do not have the ability to receive it. This raises a question. Does a person who is not saved have the ability to know the truth?

This question has been debated in theological circles for centuries. While the answer has eluded many scholars, it is very simple. James, in his epistle clearly stated that someone can believe the facts about Jesus Christ and still not be saved, "You believe that God is one. You do well; the demons also believe, and shudder" (James 2:19). Few would argue that demons are part of God's family. Yet they know who God is. They also know some things about God's attributes and, therefore, tremble. So, we conclude that salvation is not the result of believing. Believing unto eternal life is the result of being born again.

One might say that if salvation is not the result of believing but believing is the result of salvation, then those who are not saved must not be saved because they cannot believe. That is not the answer John gave in his Gospel. He quoted Jesus, "For God so loved the world, that He gave His only begotten Son, that whoever believes in Him should not perish, but have eternal life" (John 3:16). This is a well-known verse. In the same context, Jesus also taught:

> And this is the judgment, that the light has come into the world, and men loved the darkness rather than the light, for their deeds were evil. For everyone who does evil hates the light, and does not come to the light lest his deeds should be exposed. (John 3:19–20)

The term translated "loved" in the passage above is *agape,* which expresses a choice. God chose to love the world and sent light into the world by which they might be saved. However, men choose to love darkness rather than light. Therefore, men have the ability to believe, but they choose not to believe. Apart from new birth, men naturally choose not to believe. Believing is not a characteristic of those who are not born again, but unbelieving is.

This same concept is repeated at the end of the verse quoted above where John wrote, ". . . but he who does not obey the Son shall not see life, but the wrath of God abides on him" (John 3:36). The Greek term translated "obey" is the verb *apatheo*. It literally means "is not persuaded." It is transliterated into the English as *apathy*. This is also a present active participle. When we apply the same principle of Greek grammar here as we saw with *believe*, we see that some people, by character, are unpersuadable.

Remember that John presented God as the self-revealing God. This is what is meant in the prologue to his Gospel (1:1–18) by the repetition of the term *Word*. God went to great lengths to reveal Himself to mankind. However, some refuse to be persuaded by His revelation for various reasons. The general reason is that men would rather remain in darkness than receive the light. John recorded that some rejected Jesus because they wanted to cling to their own interpretation of the Bible rather than interpreting it as God had intended (John 5:16). Others wanted someone who would be their earthly king and defeat their enemies, the Romans (John 6:15). Still others did not want to lose their positions in society; they feared men more than they feared God (John 12:43).

An interesting dialogue took place between Jesus and the Jews in John 8:31–59. This dialogue marks the zenith of John's Gospel and his explanation of why some who believe receive eternal life and others do not. In verse 30 John refers to many who came to beleive in Jesus. The Greek verb translated "believe" is a point action verb, not a present active participle. Therefore, believing for them was temporary. The verb in verse 31 translated "had believed" is a grammatical construction I have not commented on thus far. Here, reference is made to believing in past time with continuing results.[11] The past time was before the time of the conversation Jesus had with them, and the present time was the moment the dialogue took place.

Note that, as the dialogue continues, those "believing" Jews begin to argue with Jesus. Eventually, they persuade themselves that Jesus could not be telling the truth. Their own arguments, which they used to refute what Jesus was teaching, overpowered their act of believing, which stemmed from what He had just taught them and what they had, at first, believed. They literally talked themselves out of believing. This is very common when discussing the plan of salvation with many non-Christians. Their own arguments become more persuasive to them than God's revelation, and so they reject the free gift of eternal life Jesus offers them. In this way, Satan blinds their eyes so that they will not believe (2 Corinthians 4:3–4). It is only when

God interrupts the process of blinding and causes the light of the glorious gospel to shine unto them that they believe (2 Corinthians 4:6).

The good news of Jesus Christ is that anyone can receive Him if they will only allow God, through His Holy Spirit and the Bible, to persuade them. Salvation does not depend upon one's ability to understand the gospel. A small child can be saved, which is a wonderful concept. It is definitely good news! No one becomes a Christian because they are smarter than someone else or because they know more than someone else. Paul wrote:

> For consider your calling, brethren, that there were not many wise according to the flesh, not many mighty, not many noble; but God has chosen the foolish things of the world to shame the wise, and God has chosen the weak things of the world to shame the things which are strong, and the base things of the world and the despised God has chosen, the things that are not, that He may nullify the things that are, that no man should boast before God. (1 Corinthians 1:26–29)

This does not exhaust all of the points that could be made regarding how someone is saved. Other thoughts, such as election and predestination are also important when discussing God's plan of salvation. Here, we have sought to explain the difference between the false gospel of Gnosticism, which limits salvation to those who have the ability to know some mysterious truth, and the true salvation of the Bible, which comes through being born again and having a personal relationship with God through Jesus Christ.

I have had the privilege of teaching on the college level for several years. I believe that it is important for me, as the instructor, to remember that knowledge and the ability to acquire it does not make one student better than another. In fact, many who have difficulty learning have difficulty because they are convinced they cannot learn. A teacher should be concerned as much with teaching *how* to learn as teaching the subject itself. A student who has come to believe he cannot learn, often is hampered by his own thoughts about himself. This builds up stress. Stress is not a good teaching tool and, in fact, hinders the learning process. Therefore, I do my best to alleviate stress while at the same time challenge the student to new heights of learning.

You, the reader, do not have to understand everything I have just said about how a person is saved. For me to say that you do, would place me in the category of a Gnostic. All you need to know is that Christ died for you and that He is alive today and wants to be both your Savior and Lord. You do not have to wait until your life changes. Any changes that come will come because of the power of God working in you, not because of your own effort. John wrote, "What He has seen and heard, of that He bears witness; and no one receives His testimony. He who has received His witness has set his seal to [this], that God is true" (John 3:32–33).

This is like signing a contract. If you believe right now that God is true, set your seal to it. Place your signature at the bottom of the page of the contract. When my wife and I bought our house, we signed our name to the contract that said we would, from then on, for the life of the contract, meet the responsibilities of that contract. We know that we have done nothing to merit salvation. We know that we can do nothing to save ourselves. We also know that we can do nothing to maintain salvation or work our way into heaven. What is important is that God's name is on the contract, whereby He promises to save us and keep us in this life and afterward to receive us into His heaven. All we are doing is signing our names under His and thereby stating that we believe it. This is what Abraham did. Paul wrote concerning Abraham,

(as it is written, "A FATHER OF MANY NATIONS HAVE I MADE YOU") in the sight of Him whom he believed, [even] God, who gives life to the dead and calls into being that which does not exist . . . and being fully assured that what He had promised, He was able also to perform. (Romans 4:17, 21)

Our signature does not save us. Even our act of believing does not save us. We are simply affirming at this moment and from now on that He is true. The affirmation might be expressed through a prayer: "Jesus, I believe in You and accept You as my Savior and Lord." This prayer will not save you, but Jesus will. We might affirm this truth by writing in our Bible, "today (month/day/year) I accepted Jesus as my Savior." Even this is not what saves us. It merely reminds us in the future of that moment when we set our seal to the truth of God.

We might also affirm the truth of God by telling someone we love and trust that we have done this. Telling them does not save us, but it will serve as a demonstration that we believe, because of a changed nature, that we have been born again. In fact, it might be helpful if you do all three. These actions will not make your salvation any more true but will help in any future moment when you might be tempted to doubt the reality of your decision.

The difference between knowing God as the result of being born again and Gnosticism is that knowing God unites us while Gnosticism divides us. It is not knowledge that divides us. It is our attitude toward each other that stems from a wrong philosophy regarding knowledge that divides us. It is the conclusions we draw about each other that divide us. When we begin to think we are better than someone else because of what we know, we have become Gnostics. When the Christian church draws the conclusion that it is better than others because of what it knows, it loses its place in society as an active part of the solution and becomes a part of the problem.

We cannot stamp out Gnosticism. Many have tried throughout history. When we think it has been eradicated, it sticks its ugly head up somewhere else. We can help to change the world by holding to a correct view of knowledge and by ceasing to play the game "I know something you don't know." We can make a difference in our neighborhoods and our schools by not playing this game. We can help those with whom we have a relationship, rather than separate ourselves from them.

CHAPTER FOUR

How We View Existence Divides Us

THE GAME: "I'VE GOT TO BE ME"

A second worldview, or philosophy, that divides us is called Existentialism. The name seems harmless enough. Like Gnosticism, it comes in all shapes and sizes. Some forms are relatively harmless, while others are very destructive. A simple definition of Existentialism is that each of us must define our own existence. A dictionary definition is:

> A philosophical and literary movement, variously religious and atheistic. . . . it is based on the doctrine that existence takes precedence over essence and holds that man is totally free and responsible for his acts, and that this responsibility is the dread and anguish that encompass him.[1]

The "dread and anguish" will be discussed later. Here the important thing to note is that Existentialism sees man as having the freedom to define his own existence.

This might seem like the perfect philosophy for today's youth. Many come into this world with little or no inherent identity because of choices their parents made before they were born or before they had any choice in the matter. Having the freedom to choose one's own identity and existence would seem to resolve the problems facing an ever-increasing population of "throwaway" children. However, it is not the positive philosophy it appears to be on the surface.

My biological parents divorced before I understood the meaning of family. Later, I was kidnapped from my mother by my paternal grandmother and transported to another part of the country. Eventually I was made ward of the court and placed in the foster-care system. As a result I was thrust into an impersonal existence where I was passed from one family of strangers to another. I was adopted at the age of eight. The turmoil and abuse in my adopted family added to the isolation and alienation I felt. Yet, when given the choice, I did not turn to Existentialism. My desire was for the more traditional existence of a stable family and a lifestyle consistent with what some now ridicule as the Beaver Cleaver existence. For me, the television families portrayed in programs such as *Leave It to Beaver* provided the positive role models I lacked in my own family.

A valid question is "Why did I choose the route I took, given so many obstacles and potholes in my path?" I believe the answer is the very reason why Existentialism is so dangerous to society. It is because no one told me that the so-called Beaver Cleaver lifestyle was a cruel hoax. No one made fun of the values and lifestyle I desired for my family and myself. That left me free to pursue traditional values unhindered. I did not choose to play the game "I've got to be me," because it had not yet become vogue and avant-garde.

Existentialism is merely an extension of Gnosticism. When we reject the knowledge of God, the next step is to reject existence as defined by God and to set about to define our own existence. Many have chosen to play the game. However, it is a losing game because the rules require paying too high a price and provide little return. Once played out, there are no winners.

Rules of the Game

Existentialism is a philosophy that has to be learned. Mankind did fine without it for most of human history. It has only been in the last two hundred years, with the rise of humanism and the decline of a belief in God, that the philosophy has been able to take hold. It is a philosophy man has devised to answer questions that stem from problems created if there is no God and if men are in full control of the universe. It has the appearance of coming from religious roots, but a closer examination proves the opposite to be true.

The man considered to be the father of modern existential thought is Søren Kierkegaard, a Danish philosopher, who wrote during the mid 1800s. Existentialism has taken on many forms since its beginning. It is generally accepted that the basic tenants of the philosophy is the absurdity of the human condition and that this absurdity alienates members of society.

Another definition of Existentialism is:

> (Existentialism is) a philosophy that emphasizes the uniqueness and isolation of the individual experience in a hostile or indifferent universe, regards human existence as unexplainable, and stresses freedom of choice and responsibility for the consequences of one's acts.[2]

Kierkegaard stressed the ambiguity and absurdity of the human situation. Concerning this, we read:

> The individual's response to this situation must be to live a totally committed life, and this commitment can only be understood by the individual who has made it. The individual therefore must always be prepared to defy the norms of society for the sake of the higher authority of a personally valid way of life. Kierkegaard ultimately advocated a "leap of faith" into a Christian way of life, which, although incomprehensible and full of risk, was the only commitment he believed could save the individual from despair.[3]

Because of the profound effect Kierkegaard's philosophy has had upon current religious thought, another view of this philosophy is in order:

> EXISTENTIALISM (exerts) a major influence on modern Protestant theology. Kierkegaard described the

various stages of existence as the aesthetic, the ethical, and the religious; advancing through this "existential dialectic," the individual becomes increasingly aware of his relationship to God. This awareness leads to despair as he realizes the antithesis between temporal existence and eternal truth. Reason is no help in achieving the final religious stage; a "leap of faith" is required.[4]

Another individual who influenced existential thought was Friedrich Nietzsche, a German philosopher who wrote during the latter part of the nineteenth century. Concerning him we read:

Nietzsche, who was not acquainted with the work of Kierkegaard, influenced subsequent existentialist thought through his criticism of traditional metaphysical and moral assumptions and through his espousal of tragic pessimism and the life-affirming individual will that opposes itself to the moral conformity of the majority.[5]

Martin Heidegger, another German philosopher who lived from 1889 to 1976, took Existentialism a step further.

Heidegger argued that humanity finds itself in an incomprehensible, indifferent world. Human beings can never hope to understand why they are here; instead, each individual must choose a goal and follow it with passionate conviction, aware of

the certainty of death and the ultimate meaningless-
ness of one's life.[6]

Some have interpreted Heidegger's "passionate conviction" to be a form of personal suicide. This is not
necessarily physical suicide that culminates in physical
death but a psychological suicide that is expressed in
one's dedication to a cause no matter how narrow or
extreme. We see this in modern-day social activism, both
inside and outside the church, as individuals engage in
marching and picketing and other forms of nonviolent
and violent protests for or against various social causes.
Through a process of cognitive deception, these individuals minimize all other points of view and maximize
their own views in order to achieve what to them is a
just balance in the world.

Winners and Losers

Existentialism is a pessimistic outlook on life. It begins with a sense of hopelessness concerning the human condition. Then it moves to the belief in the
alienation of the individual from others and society in
general. Listen to the lyrics of most secular music,
whether it is country western, rock and roll, blues, jazz,
rap, or acid rock. The basic theme is negative. Which
came first: existentialist philosophy or secular lyrics?
Beyond a doubt, the philosophy of Existentialism came
first. In fact, almost the entire entertainment industry
feeds on the pessimism of Existentialism, yet hardly ever
uses the word.

A similar correlation exists between Existentialism and the rise of political activism in Western culture. There is a sense in which World War I, the Great Depression, followed by World War II robbed society of any hope that there could ever be a lasting peace. The rise of Communism in Europe, the partitioning of Eastern Europe behind the Iron Curtain, and the subsequent Cold War drained away much of the optimism that came with the dawn of the twentieth century. Those of us old enough to remember watched as the philosophy began to permeate college and university campuses in the 1960s and 1970s. The new battlefield was the mind and soul of the youth of Western culture. Victory would go to the philosophy that could capture enough souls. Existentialism won.

At first, the "I've got to be me" war cry of Existentialism came from liberal college and university campuses in the form of the free-speech movement. Then, it was the hippie and drug culture and the sexual revolution. Focusing on the belief that the world was absurd, the gospel of Existentialism was the invitation to do your own thing, define your own existence, seek your own relevance. The biggest losers in all of that were wholesome relationships and meaningful communication between social groups.

Since the allies claimed victory at the end of World War II, war was fought though never declared in Korea. With both sides stalemated at the demilitarized zone, and with no clear victory, any sense of nationalistic pride or identity was lost. Failure to reach a peace agreement at Panmunjom left both sides in a state of perpetual war. To this day, the demilitarized zone stands as a symbol of the failure of modern society.

Then came the quagmire called Vietnam. It possessed all of the elements of the Korean conflict. In the minds of many, Vietnam was a small country with little relevance to Western civilization. It represented a battle line between Communism and capitalism. Those who controlled the war did so from the comfort and security of their own communities far from the bloody battlefields. The army called upon to fight that war was made up of youth already steeped in existential philosophy. They had been taught to question the right of the military-industrial complex to control their lives and to send them off to their deaths in an undeclared war. The youth believed they had a right to define their existence for themselves and to question the relevance of the war to that existence.

The passive resistance and civil disobedience of Mahatma Gandhi and others fit in well with existentialist philosophy and became the weapons of choice against the injustices of a society from which the youth were more and more alienated. The Civil Rights movement also adopted the same weapons in its war against an unjust society.

The battle cry became "Down with the establishment—any establishment." The attitude was "Don't trust anyone over thirty." The rising counterculture took up many causes. With the sympathy of the media, many found personal power through this philosophy. Their very existence was defined by the political causes they espoused.

With the passing of time, Existentialism moved off the college campuses and into the public school system, into the halls of justice and government, and into every facet of life. As a generation steeped in this philosophy grew older, it moved into the boardrooms of cooperate America, into the advertising industry, and into the entertainment industry. Existentialism next moved into the neighborhoods of suburban America in the form of political action groups. Finally, it moved into Evangelical churches through such organizations as the Moral Majority, the Right to Life organization, the Christian Coalition, and other politically oriented groups. Political protests with civil disobedience and passive resistance were the weapons of choice of the existential movement. And they became the weapons of choice of Evangelical churches fighting abortion and other causes deemed harmful to society.

Many may object to equating the political strategies of the religious right with that of the secular left and to identifying both as the fallout of Existentialism. Yet consider the overarching philosophy of both extremes. Both are driven by a sense that society in general has failed and that individual members and groups within society are alienated from each other. Both see the exercise of individual freedom of choice as their inalienable right and that each individual must choose a goal and follow it with passionate conviction. What earlier existentialists identified as angst, or a pessimistic generalized anxiety, has become the oil that fuels the fires of both the right and left wings of the political and religious spectrum of society. Both extremes espouse a form of tragic pessimism and the life-affirming, individual will that opposes itself to the moral conformity of the majority.

This does not mean that all Christians fit into the category of the far left or the right wings of the political spectrum. Those who do not fit are criticized and even ostracized by those who do fit into this spectrum. The result is that political fervor is often substituted for religious fervor, the loser being the gospel of Jesus Christ. Christianity is now commonly viewed as a sect more bent on judging the world than presenting Christ as the Savior of the world. The steadying appeal of the Bible to set our minds on "the things that make for peace" (Luke 19:42) has been drowned out by the louder voices calling for a heightened awareness of angst coupled with a sense of outrage as the great unifying and motivating force to bring about change in society—regardless of what that might be.

Along with the slow march of Existentialism, as it won the soul of most of a generation, an almost imperceptible transformation took place. Many of the causes espoused by one group or another were very honorable in the beginning, and progress toward positive change took place. Originally, Existentialism was more of a tool for change than a lifestyle to be lived. However, gradually it became a way of life with or without a just cause to champion. When progress was made and change had taken place, many caught up in the tide of Existentialism sought another cause in order to stay in business.

While not every minority person has gained as much as he or she should have, and while not every woman has broken through the glass ceiling in corporate America, and while not every snail darter has been rescued from oblivion from runaway dam construction, progress has been achieved. But the victor was Existentialism. So, now what is society to do with the angry "In your face," "Your wrong, I'm right," "I've got to be me," "Do your own thing" tool for social change? The answer is that you package it, market it, and sell it to a new generation that does not have the faintest idea what it was all about in the first place.

Existentialism, like its close cousin *dialectical materialism*, with its thesis, antithesis, and synthesis, was and is a philosophy of revolution. Its goal is to produce change. In the process of trying to change the world, Existentialism has not made society a better place to live. Groups with opposing views have not come together in the grand new society that was suppose to be the synthesis of the great dialectical materialism. Consider the geographical and cultural climate of Columbine High, Jefferson County, Colorado. There is no more diverse place to live in the United States than the neighborhood where that tragic drama unfolded.

Littleton, Colorado, and the greater Denver area, is no different than many other metropolitan areas in the United States. However, the extremes of diversity fostered by Existentialism are more readily seen because of the ruggedness of the landscape and extremes of climate. Colorado has become the playground of existentialists. A few years ago, my wife and I visited a church in Colorado that was supposed to be conservative. In his sermon, the pastor called the account of creation in Genesis "The Big Bang Theory." The birth of Jesus was the "Little Bang Theory." I resisted the urge to walk out, because I wanted to find out how far he would go. His solution for saving society was to rid ourselves of Eurocentric, male-dominated religion and return to worshipping God in the buffalo.

The problem was not that he was teaching what he believed, the problem was that he was presenting what he believed as true Christianity. He set himself up as a teacher of a truth far different than the truth taught in the Bible. He invited others to join him in redefining existence to suit themselves.

Please understand, I am not saying that Colorado has a corner on existentialist thought. What I am saying is that Columbine High is located in an area of the world where this morbid philosophy has found fertile soil. The community that tolerated this preacher's thoughts consists of many whose names we would find in the postscripts of major movies, television programs, and on CDs at the top of the charts in the recording industry. Through their influence, our children are caught in the crushing grip of Existentialism like meat in a meat grinder. Littleton, Colorado, is an excellent example of what is happening everywhere in America.

Whether they live in Littleton, Colorado, or Peoria, American youth are the targets of a negative, destructive worldview. Whether they wear trench coats and play video games or wear shoulder pads on the football field, the "I've got to be me" game is being played with tragic results. As each succeeding generation bears the scars of existentialist thinking, society is caught in a downward spiral that increases in speed exponentially. It has not become simply a philosophy of despair but a philosophy of destruction. Postmodernism, with its political-correctness police, is merely the logical extension of Existentialism and can correctly be viewed as neoExistentialism.

Perhaps the most frustrating side of this human philosophy, regardless of the form it takes, is that it is so negative, so pointless, and so powerless. The more men ask questions while refusing to seek answers through what God has already revealed (Romans 1:18*ff*), the more hopeless man's existence seems. Think of the contradictions of this philosophy. Many children today grow up in suburban America with three cars in the garage and homes better equipped than most palaces throughout human history. They have access to more knowledge and have the freedom to explore life more than at any time since man was driven from the Garden of Eden. You would think they could find happiness in all of this. I believe that if it were not for the destructive philosophy of Existentialism, they would find happiness. But Existentialism poisons the mind so that the sunshine of joy cannot penetrate life.

With all of the physical comforts of modern society has come a gloom that is baffling, until we look closely at what society is serving up as a regular diet. A lot of attention has been focused on the video games that the shooters at Columbine High played hour after hour.

There can be little doubt that these played a part in the motivation to kill as many of their classmates as they could. The thrill of killing other human beings could not have been the only motivation behind the shooting. There had to be a sense of hopelessness, of despair that things could ever get better, of personal alienation more profound than words can describe. Those boys were not stupid. They had to know that by killing others they were killing themselves. Their suicide was both philosophical and physical—the final solution to an absurd existence defined by Existentialism.

Whether or not they ever heard the word *Existentialism*, the behavior they carried out on that fateful day was an existential act as much as any single act could be. It was a lashing out at other people and society in general as if they were the cause of the despair those two boys were feeling. Any act of such magnitude is the culmination of unhealthy and broken relationships, cognitive dissonance taken to the highest degree, Gnostic laughing in your face, individual existence finally being defined as absurdity beyond absurdity. Yet their physical suicide is no more real and indicative of the existence they chose than are the countless psychological and philosophical suicides committed every day by individuals who choose to define their own existence at the expense of relationships, truth, and God's reality, over which He alone has sway.

We all come to a place in our lives when it seems as if we are looking into a black hole that invites us to throw ourselves into it and be swallowed up by its darkness.

Yet most of us come to our senses and realize that the black hole only exists in our minds. There is a rainbow after the storm. There is life after personal failure and disappointment. This is true, however, only if we are not staring into a dark abyss prepared for us by some warped minds who feel that the sense of vertigo while hanging over the abyss is somehow a better reality than the sunlight after the storm clouds have passed.

The greatest danger from existential thinking is that we begin to think that the reality created in our minds, or prepared for us through technology, is more real than God's reality. I feel so fortunate that I was not introduced to existential thought when I was searching for my identity and existence as a youth. Had I bowed my knee to the god of Existentialism, he surely would have destroyed me. The false gospel of Existentialism says, "Trust me." It beckons, "I will make your life real." Yet the end result is total defeat and, if allowed to happen, total annihilation of existence from a human perspective. Existentialism is not the construction of existence; it is the destruction of existence—God's existence.

Refusing to Play the Game: "I've Got to Be Me"

I remember the night I reached out to take hold of God's reality. I was attending a servicemen's retreat while in the Navy. There were a number of very powerful speakers, men who knew how to excite the emotions. Yet mine was not an emotional experience. In fact, to be sure it was not; I separated myself from the rest of the group and went off by myself. If God was real and was offering me a choice to receive His reality, I wanted to be sure it was a transaction between Him and me and not the persuasive speeches of men or the fickleness of emotion. There were a lot of things that needed to be changed in my life, and no one less than the Sovereign God of the universe was going to be able to make those changes.

I was not looking for some way to change myself or to somehow create a new existence. If Christ did not come into my life that night, I had no existence—at least, not that I wanted to live in. Yet it was not the thought of suicide that was pulling me up to God. It was the hope that His reality would be better than any I had created up to that point or that anyone else had created for me. What I believed I needed to do was grasp hold of His reality. I did that by praying a simple prayer. I waited for some time to see how I felt about that decision before telling anyone about it. I wanted to be sure it was real.

This is how I have approached most of the decisions I have made with reference to my relationship with God. I wait to see how I feel about it the next morning. Unlike many foolish experiences, such as waking up with a hangover or worse, I have found that the morning brings new joy and that the decision the night before was the correct decision, even if it was made in desperation. I learned this long before I read Jeremiah's words:

> I have become a laughingstock to all my people,
> their [mocking] song all the day. He has filled me with

bitterness, He has made me drunk with wormwood. And He has broken my teeth with gravel; He has made me cower in the dust. My soul has been rejected from peace; I have forgotten happiness. So I say, "My strength has perished, and [so has] my hope from the LORD." Remember my affliction and my wandering, the wormwood and bitterness. Surely my soul remembers and is bowed down within me. *This I recall to my mind, therefore I have hope. The LORD's lovingkindness indeed never cease, for His compassions never fail. [They] are new every morning; great is Thy faithfulness. "The LORD is my portion," says my soul, "Therefore I have hope in Him."* (Lamentations 3:14–24, italics mine)

Many who begin the Christian life, begin with the misunderstanding that they have to make it work. Like the existentialist, they set out to recreate their own existence. After all, doesn't the Bible say we are to be conformed into the image of Christ (Romans 8:29)? The process of being conformed to His image is not our responsibility. To believe it is our responsibility is a false view of Christianity and, like its cousin Existentialism, will lead to defeat and despair. The Gnostic, the existentialist, the modernist, and the postmodernist are all wrong and so is a Christianity that teaches or implies that we have to somehow define our own existence.

Toward the end of the first century, John encouraged his readers in the church with these words:

See how great a love the Father has bestowed upon us, that we would be called children of God; and [such] we are. For this reason the world does not know us, because it did not know Him. Beloved, now we are children of God, and it has not appeared as yet what we shall be. We know that, when He appears, we shall be like Him, because we shall see Him just as He is. And everyone who has this hope [fixed] on Him purifies himself, just as He is pure. (1 John 3:1–3)

No one has the power to create or recreate existence or reality. In Christ, we receive the ability to appropriate God's reality. The process of appropriating His reality is through studying His Word while under the power of the Holy Spirit. The message of His Word transforms our lives from within. The change is often imperceptible at first. The writer of the Book of Hebrews noted:

> For the word of God is living and active and sharper than any two-edged sword, and piercing as far as the division of soul and spirit, of both joints and marrow, and able to judge the thoughts and intentions of the heart. (Hebrews 4:12)

I was blessed with good counsel at the beginning of my relationship with Jesus Christ. I was encouraged to memorize Scripture. Some of the verses suggested to me have become a part of my reality as God has allowed me to experience it.

> Wherewithal shall a young man cleanse his way? by taking heed thereto according to thy word. . . . Thy word have I hid in mine heart, that I might not sin against thee. (Psalm 119:9, 11, KJV)

Blessed is the man that walketh not in the counsel of the ungodly, nor standeth in the way of sinners, nor sitteth in the seat of the scornful. But his delight is in the law of the LORD; and in his law doth he meditate day and night. And he shall be like a tree planted by the rivers of water, that bringeth forth his fruit in his season; his leaf also shall not wither; and whatsoever he doeth shall prosper. (Psalm 1:1–3, KJV)

Therefore if any man be in Christ, he is a new creature: old things are passed away; behold, all things are become new. (2 Corinthians 5:17, KJV)

And this is the record, that God hath given to us eternal life, and this life is in his Son. He that hath the Son hath life; and he that hath not the Son of God hath not life. (John 5:11–12, KJV)

Each of these verses and more became my reality as I memorized them and prayed through them. I do not mean to imply that all of the storm clouds of life and all of my problems disappeared immediately. I continued to struggle and, at times, continue to struggle today. However, God's Word is a beacon in the storms of life. If I stray too far from Christ, its beams guide me back to safety.

Years later, after college and two stints in seminary, with a master's degree and a doctorate—both in pastoral studies and Bible—and twelve years of pastoral ministry, I still fell into the trap of trying to define my own existence. This is a constant danger, even for Christians.

We become so zealous for the things of God that we set out to create His reality through the arm of our flesh. It is a difficult thing to distinguish between fleshly effort and Spirit control. Yet that is exactly what God's Word is suppose to do when we simply study it.

One day, I found myself reflecting on the struggles of the Christian life as I was studying the Book of Ephesians. In Ephesians 4:17–24, Paul wrote:

> So this I say, and affirm together with the Lord, that you walk no longer just as the Gentiles also walk, in the futility of their mind, being darkened in their understanding, excluded from the life of God because of the ignorance that is in them, because of the hardness of their heart; and they, having become callous, have given themselves over to sensuality for the practice of every kind of impurity with greediness. But you did not learn Christ in this way, if indeed you have heard Him and have been taught in Him, just as truth is in Jesus, that, in reference to your former manner of life, you lay aside the old self, which is being corrupted in accordance with the lusts of deceit, and that you be renewed in the spirit of your mind, and put on the new self, which in [the likeness of] God has been created in righteousness and holiness of the truth.

That particular day, I felt as if my life was the product of the futility of my mind. The battle for Christ seemed to be a losing one, especially in my own life and ministry. Then I noticed the strange way the last sentence was phrased in the original language. The command was to put on, through the renewing of the spirit of my mind, the new self, "Which . . . *has been created* in righteousness and holiness of the truth" (Italics mine).

The problem was that, without knowing it, I was still trying to create my own existence when all I needed to do was accept the existence God had already created for me. The tense of the Greek verb translated "has been created" suggests that a person who has truly been born again has been recreated already.[7] This renewing of the spirit of the mind comes through appropriating what God has already accomplished through Christ.

The true Christian experience, new life in Christ, accomplishes what Existentialism with all of its high mindedness attempts to do. It redefines one's existence. However, the agent of the change and the power to change is God's, not ours. The existence is His existence, which He provides in Christ. Through the power of the Holy Spirit, as we study His Word, we begin to think like God thinks and so are able to put on His reality. As the reality of God becomes clearer and clearer through careful examination of the Bible, we discover who we are in Christ and who we are in relation to others in Christ's Body, the church. This clarity comes from accurately interpreting Scripture.

Unfortunately, many prominent church leaders today advocate an existential approach to Bible interpretation by which God's reality is obscured and the message of Scripture is given a decidedly existential slant. They no longer use the nomenclature of the liberalism of the past. They now couch their existentialist philosophy in language more acceptable to Evangelical Christianity.

Sometimes the difference between the true message of Scripture and the distorted message of existentialists served up as truth is almost imperceptible. This is why we must be diligent in our pursuit of the truth of the Bible. In the first-century church, when persecution became almost unbearable, God's message was not "create your own existence." Peter made this very clear in his first epistle. We do not find the angst of Existentialism in this letter to a persecuted church. Instead we find joy and hope both in this life and the life to come.

To find that joy and hope, those persecuted believers were encouraged to take to the true message of Scripture like a baby takes to a bottle of warm milk (1 Peter 2:2). They were reminded of their unity in Christ as "a CHOSEN RACE, a ROYAL PRIESTHOOD, a HOLY NATION, a PEOPLE FOR [God's] OWN POSSESSION . . . (who) once were NOT a PEOPLE, but now you are THE PEOPLE OF GOD; you had NOT RECEIVED MERCY, but now you have RECEIVED MERCY" (1 Peter 2:9–10).

It is ironic that so many persecuted Christians around the world are accepting the true reality of God while the church in America, wealthy beyond comprehension, is turning away from the truth to the false hope of Existentialism. These existentialists are trying to create their own contrived unity rather than acknowledging the genuine unity that God alone creates through His Word and the power of the Holy Spirit.

The writer of the Book of Hebrews exhorted us:

Since therefore, brethren, we have confidence to enter the holy place by the blood of Jesus, by a new and living way which He inaugurated for us through the veil, that is, His flesh, and since [we have] a great priest over the house of God, let us draw near with a sincere heart in full assurance of faith, having our hearts sprinkled [clean] from an evil conscience and our bodies washed with pure water. Let us hold fast the confession of our hope without wavering, for He who promised is faithful; and let us consider how to stimulate one another to love and good deeds, not forsaking our own assembling together, as is the habit of some, but encouraging [one another;] and all the more, as you see the day drawing near. (Hebrews 10:19–25)

This is nothing short of a call to the existence that God has already provided for us in a local church setting. Our task is to find a local church that believes the Bible and practices what it teaches. There is no room for Existentialism in the family of God. There is no need for it, because He has made very clear what our existence is and what our responsibilities are in this existence.

What is wonderful about being a Christian is that the Bible does not lead us into a hopeless existence that alienates us from others. That sense of hopelessness and alienation comes from the existence of someone who is not a child of God. Existentialists are correct in one thing: People apart from God are alienated, and their lives are hopeless. Paul described existence apart from God:

Therefore remember, that formerly you, the Gentiles in the flesh, who are called "Uncircumcision"

by the so-called "Circumcision," [which is] performed in the flesh by human hands—[remember]
that you were at that time separate from Christ, excluded from the commonwealth of Israel, and strangers to the covenants of promise, having no hope and
without God in the world. (Ephesians 2:11–12)

The language is Jewish in tone, but the meaning is
the same. Without God, life is meaningless and people
are alienated from each other. In Christ, however, God
provides us with an existence in relationship to Him, a
life of purpose and fulfillment, and a hope both in this
life and the next. In God's reality, there is already unity.

But now in Christ Jesus you who formerly were
far off have been brought near by the blood of Christ.
For He Himself is our peace, who made both [groups
into] one and broke down the barrier of the dividing
wall, by abolishing in His flesh the enmity, [which is]
the Law of commandments [contained] in ordinances,
that in Himself He might make the two into one new
man, [thus] establishing peace, and might reconcile
them both in one body to God through the cross, by it
having put to death the enmity. AND HE CAME AND
PREACHED PEACE TO YOU WHO WERE FAR AWAY, AND PEACE TO
THOSE WHO WERE NEAR; for through Him we both have
our access in one Spirit to the Father. So then you are
no longer strangers and aliens, but you are fellow citi-
zens with the saints, and are of God's household, having been built upon the foundation of the apostles and
prophets, Christ Jesus Himself being the corner [stone]
in whom the whole building, being fitted together is

growing into a holy temple in the Lord, in whom you also are being built together into a dwelling of God in the Spirit. (Ephesians 2:13–22)

A good study to help us avoid the pitfalls of Existentialism is to follow the *one anothers* in the New Testament epistles. Dr. Gene Getz has written a delightful book titled, *Building Up One Another.*[8] Using his book as a guide, you will discover both the responsibilities and the blessing of God's reality. There is much we can learn about the existence called "in Christ."[9] Paul's desire was that we come to a full realization of its privileges and responsibilities. He wrote:

[I pray that] the eyes of your heart may be enlightened, so that you may know what is the hope of His calling, what are the riches of the glory of His inheritance in the saints, and what is the surpassing greatness of His power toward us who believe. [These are] in accordance with the working of the strength of His might which He brought about in Christ, when He raised Him from the dead and seated Him at His right hand in the heavenly [places], far above all rule and authority and power and dominion, and every name that is named, not only in this age, but also in the one to come. (Ephesians 1:18–21)

Christians do not have to set about defining their own existence. God has already done this. What we need to do is appropriate God's reality with its privileges and responsibilities along with the power of the Holy Spirit and His instructions from His guidebook, the Bible. We cannot change the tide of history as society rushes into the abyss of its own making through Existentialism, but we can change the tide in our own lives and in the lives of our children. We can and we must, or we will suffer the same destruction as others who are blinded by this evil philosophy from Satan.

CHAPTER FIVE

How We View Behavior Divides Us

THE GAME: "THE DEVIL MADE ME DO IT"

Perhaps the most baffling question lingering from the shooting at Columbine High in Littleton, Colorado, is why those boys chose to do what they did, killing and maiming so many people. Some blame the Internet, some the entertainment industry, some the video games, some the National Rifle Association, some the parents of the shooters, and on and on. Under the surface of the blame game is the basic philosophy that the shooters were products of their environment. If we could somehow change the environment, we would do away with those acts of violence.

I call that game "The devil made me do it," not because people believe in a real devil and blame him but because they are simply seeking a scapegoat. Another name for this game is *Behaviorism*. It is a belief system that places much of the blame for destructive behavior on the environment or on genetic makeup. Behaviorism as a philosophy divides us because it teaches that individuals are not morally responsible for their behavior. Yet accepting responsibility for one's actions is the very thing needed for healthy relationships in society.

Behaviorism is "a movement in psychology that advocates the use of strict experimental procedures to study observable behavior (or responses) in relation to the environment (or stimuli)."[1] Behaviorism seeks to discover why people behave the way they do. In its simplest form, it seeks to examine through observation the cause and effect of behavior and then to draw conclusions that can be used to alter that behavior.

I call it a game because, on the one hand, behaviorists have been able to identify certain behavior patterns and their causes yet, on the other hand, they also have become adept at controlling human behavior. To see how effective Behaviorism is, we need to consider the advertising industry and its ability to sell almost anything. This ability comes from conclusions drawn by behaviorists, who study human behavior. Behaviorists are quick to deny that they are to blame for destructive behavior that stems from products sold using methods devised by the techniques they have developed. Behaviorism is more than the scientific study of human behavior. It has become a philosophy because it is based upon some basic presuppositions that do not belong in the field of scientific investigation. Those presuppositions, such as morality, cannot be put into a test tube and measured.

Rules of the Game

One of the most powerful tools in the hands of behaviorists in the past forty years has been the television. As technology moved from a tiny black-and-white screen with a grainy image to large living-color images today, the subject matter moved from simple programs promoting virtue and the better life, to sex, violence, and every form of debauchery imaginable. A standard format for prime-time viewing is the sitcom in which every deviant behavior is presented as normal and anything virtuous is mocked. Even when a viewer is selective in the programs he watches, the programming is interrupted with juicy tidbits of decadence under the guise of commercial advertising.

Other forms of technology are catching up to television and even merging with it, such as satellite technology, the computer, virtual-reality video games, and the Internet. There is no end to what can be done to motivate and manipulate a society of consumers drunk on every kind of voyeurism and seductive behavior. This is all served up as free speech, entertainment, and artistic creativity. How effective are the techniques learned from the study of human behavior? Observe the sale of toys at Christmas time. Observe the dress and behavior of youth on the school grounds. Someone is very good at controlling human behavior by creating a desire for the latest fad.

Any time there is an outcry that television, movies, and computers have become the purveyors of much of what is wrong in society, they are defended as expressions of art and free speech protected by the First Amendment. Adults and children alike defend their right to watch and/or portray any human activity no matter how degrading and damaging to society. Some argue that it is a harmless expression of human freedom. Yet those who produce and market the material pay millions of dollars a minute simply for the privilege of hocking their wares at times when they know millions of people will be watching. If they did not believe in the effectiveness of Behaviorism, they would not be spending so much money on this method of marketing.

Not all marketing is harmful. In fact, the lifestyle of Americans coveted and copied by the rest of the world would be impossible without the effectiveness of behavioral psychology. Capitalism and the free-market society depend upon Behaviorism to create the desire to buy the products that keep the economy moving and consumers consuming. Even the Christian community utilizes principles of behavioral psychology to market the gospel. Behaviorism has become so pervasive in everyday life that it is difficult to tell whether the behavior observed is caused by natural environmental factors or by artificial factors created by behavioral psychologists and injected into the environment.

Society has become schizophrenic with reference to human behavior. When there is a product to sell or a profit to be made, marketers run to behaviorists to find out how to package the product and entice the consumer to buy it. On the other hand, when a product, such as a violent video game or a movie, is suggested as a contributing factor to antisocial behavior, the same marketers who packaged the product to sell it deny any culpability in the cause of the antisocial behavior. It seems that as long as there is a profit to be made, Behaviorism is a valid philosophy. However, the moment Behaviorism is accused of being part of the problem, behaviorists refuse to accept any of the blame.

The Development of Behaviorism as a Philosophy

Behaviorism is a recent philosophy. By recent, I mean within the last one hundred and fifty years. Its rise parallels the rise of psychology in Western culture. To understand Behaviorism as a philosophy, we need to understand its development from its origin as a division of psychology called *behavioral psychology*. Psychology is a study of the soul. The name comes from the Greek word *psuche* transliterated into the English with the suffix *ology,* meaning "a study of." Some Christians reject psychology as a valid discipline. Some even see it as evil. However, in its simplest form, it is merely a study of the human soul.

Usually, when Christians think of soul they think of the immaterial part of man that continues after physical death. When we study the development of the concept in the Bible from the standpoint of the progress of revelation, we see that such a meaning is not found in the Old Testament but was added in the New Testament. Much confusion has arisen from the failure to see the development of the concept of *psuche* from its Old Testament roots in the use of the Hebrew term *nepes.*

Time and space do not allow for a full discussion of *psuche* here. However, Lawrence O. Richards provides a succinct explanation that will help to explain the connection between the biblical concept of soul and its use in the discipline of psychology:

> "Soul" in the OT, then, does not indicate some immaterial part of human beings that continues after death. *Nepes* essentially means life as it is uniquely experienced by personal beings. Each human being is unique and precious. *Nepes* also implies that the meaning of human life cannot be summed up in what happens to the physical body. One can be rich or poor, have success or failure, and live in times of peace or war. But what makes us unique is our rich inner life, virtually interacting with and shaping external circumstances by our drives, will, and emotions.[2]

This view of soul is consistent with many New Testament occurrences of the Greek term *psuche*. One reference in the New Testament that underscores the meaning of soul is found in John 10:11, where Jesus says, "I am the good shepherd; the good shepherd lays down His life [*psuche*] for the sheep." Jesus did not simply give up His physical body to death at the end of His life. He gave up for a season the privileges and benefits that He possessed as God from eternity past, to come to earth and take on the form of a man.

Another reference that demonstrates the important correlation between *soul* and *life* is John 12:25, "He who loves his life [*psuche*] loses it, and he who hates his life

[*psuche*] in this world shall keep it to life [*zoe*] eternal."
We can see that Larry Richardson's explanation of *psuche*
above is an accurate clarification of the association between the biblical concept of *soul* and the meaning of
the term *psychology*.

The underlining assumption of psychology is that
one can observe the soul by observing the actions of
the person. Such observations would give the observer
a picture of the person's motives, attitudes, and desires. This assumption is consistent with several statements in the New Testament. One such passage is
found in Matthew:

> You will know them by their fruits. Grapes are not
> gathered from thorn [bushes] nor figs from thistles,
> are they? Even so, every good tree bears good fruit,
> but the bad tree bears bad fruit. A good tree cannot
> produce bad fruit, nor can a bad tree produce good
> fruit. (Matthew 7:16–18)

When a philosophy is based upon false presuppositions, its conclusions regarding life and existence are
false. In the above quote, if good fruit is called bad and
bad fruit good, then the ultimate conclusion regarding
the tree will be false. This is exactly why the philosophy of Behaviorism is false.

False Presuppositions of Behaviorists

The picture gleaned by behavioral psychologists
when they observe human behavior may or may not be

accurate. Accuracy depends upon the actual correlation between the behavior and the motives of the individual. Accuracy also depends upon the skill of the observer. The greatest weakness of behavioral psychology as a disciplined study of the human soul is the false presuppositions regarding the soul so prevalent today.

Behaviorism began as a blend of physiology and psychology. One of the first proponents of Behaviorism was the American psychologist John B. Watson who was influenced by the Russian physiologists Ivan P. Pavlov and Vladimir M. Bekhterev. These two individuals are noted for their studies of the conditioning of animals. Also influencing Behaviorism is the rise of humanism, with its rejection of God and the supernatural. Another influence is the wide acceptance of evolution, with its view of man as simply another species in the animal kingdom.

The merging of physiology and psychology into Behaviorism was based on the premise that humans would behave the same way as animals given the right external stimulus. One early researcher was B. F. Skinner, who was known for his experiments on animals and humans. One popular experiment during World War II was the training of pigeons to peck at the crosshairs of a bombsight when a visual connection was made between the picture of the bombsight and food dropping into its cage. This branch of psychology became known as stimulus-response psychology or behavioral psychology.

Behaviorism, as a philosophy, governs the thinking of almost every facet of society, from the public school system to the workplace to the marketplace to entertainment. One of the common practices of behaviorists is called *behavior modification,* where an attempt is made to change the behavior of individuals by changing some elements in their environment.

Abraham Maslow and the Hierarchy of Needs

One of the best-known behavioral psychologists was Abraham Harold Maslow, a leading exponent of humanistic psychology. He believed that too much emphasis in psychology was directed toward aberrant behavior and the modification of such behavior. Instead, he chose to spend his time focusing on human motivation. It is his teachings on motivation that most influences society today.

Maslow devised the theory called the *hierarchy of needs* (see diagram 5 on the next page). He posited seven categories of needs and then ranked the categories in ascending order from the lowest to the highest, with the lowest being the greater need. He theorized that the greater needs—he called them *prepotent* needs—lower on the list must be met before the lesser needs higher on the list could be addressed. He also theorized that meeting the greater needs below and then moving up the list could induce human motivation. Conversely, a need further up the scale could not be addressed until a lower, or more prepotent need, had been met.

How prevalent Maslow's theory of the hierarchy of needs has become is seen in a reference to it in a manual used to train electrical apprentices who are studying to

DIAGRAM 5

Maslow's Hierarchy of Needs

be journeymen electricians. In the introductory information for the lesson titled "Orientation Keys to Success: Motivation and Leadership" the student is instructed:

This lesson will lead the student through a study of why people behave and react the way that they do. The nature of your chosen career will bring you into contact with many people with whom you must work. The ability to work with others in harmony while being productive is an important factor to you and your employer. Knowing about the levels of human needs and basic theories of motivation and leadership will make you more valuable to yourself, your employer and your industry.[3]

The writers of the lesson plan then go on to diagram Maslow's hierarchy of needs. In their diagram, the most prepotent needs, those that take priority over all other needs, are "The need for food, shelter, sleep, sex, clothing, water."[4] These needs correspond with what Maslow labeled "Physiological needs." We will come back to the definition of the basic foundational needs in the next section. However, it is important to recognize the implications of such a statement. Basically, the theory says that this basic category of needs must be met before a person will be motivated to seek fulfillment of the needs at the next higher level. In Maslow's hierarchy the next level would be safety needs or, according to the apprenticeship manual, "The need for ordered existence and a secure future."[5]

The manual goes on to explain that other behaviorists have suggested their own list of hierarchical needs. However, the basic philosophy, that behavior and motivation can be predetermined by manipulating the environment, is the underlining premise of all of these theories and a basic presumption of this training manual.

This demonstrates how prevalent Behaviorism has become as a philosophy of life. It is the basic philosophy of much of public education. It is the philosophy behind many laws and government regulations. The judicial system, including the penal system, resorts to Behaviorism for its judgments and subsequent sentencing.

I was first introduced to the concept of the hierarchy of needs as a new Christian in college while studying for a degree in education. The theory, which was presented as irrefutable fact at the time, implied to me that much of my sinful behavior, which I sincerely wanted to overcome, was the result of environmental factors. My physical appetites were preprogrammed, and no matter how hard I tried, I would not be able to move up the hierarchy scale until those appetites were satisfied. Behavioral psychologists, were telling me my behavior was not fully under my control because it was motivated by forces beyond my control. This was not good news to me. It meant that there was little hope of overcoming some very bad habits I had developed early in my life.

Since then, behaviorists have moderated their philosophy somewhat. In all fairness to the apprenticeship manual referred to above, the writer notes the dilemma Maslow's theory presents since it does not prove to be correct in practice. The manual continues:

> So, all you have to do to motivate a person is to look at their needs! Not exactly. The difficulty with Maslow's hierarchy is that you cannot use the hierarchy to predict a person's behavior. The starving sculptor will freeze in a lonely studio and go without food in order to complete a piece of sculpture. His priority need is esteem or self-fulfillment and not the more basic needs. The *"independent"* is another example. A journeyman that holds on to a work method in defiance of everyone else in the crew is a worker whose need for self-esteem has a priority over social need.

He/she is more concerned about ego and self-image than belonging to the majority.[6] (Italics mine)

"Independent" here would be the non-union contractor who refuses to abide by the same motivating forces of a union worker. The dilemma of this decidedly union-minded writer is that he is unable to use the theory to control someone who does not want to be controlled. It is an admission that mankind is more complex than the behaviorists originally theorized. What appears to be true in the animal kingdom is far less compelling when applied to humans. However, we must not take comfort from this observation. Notice the conclusion drawn from the fact that the "independent" cannot be motivated or controlled by simple manipulation of his environment. Such a person is viewed as defiant, egotistical, having a wrong self-image and being unwilling to conform to the majority.

Behaviorism and Postmodernism

Here is where Behaviorism becomes very dangerous. At first, the purpose of studying human behavior was simply to find out why humans behave the way they do. Then the goal was to learn how to change behavior by changing the environment. Then Behaviorism began to ascribe value to behavior, seeking to curtail some behavior while encouraging other behavior. At that point, personal ethics and social mores enter into the choice of which behavior to encourage and which to discourage. Finally, the behaviorist sits in judgment upon certain behavior as harmful to society while ascribing value to other behavior based upon a philosophical grid the behaviorist adopts. It is easy to see then how the threefold philosophies concerning knowledge, existence, and behavior merge to form a formidable tool for social change and/or a tool to prevent change in the directions deemed inappropriate to the philosophers.

When postmodernists see people as cogs in a social machine, who "are the product of their culture and only imagine they are self-governing . . . [that] there is no such thing as objective rationality [that is, reasons unaffected by bias]," they are taking Behaviorism to its next logical step. The god of modernism is human thought. The god of postmodernism is culture as determined by behaviorists. Human behavior that does not conform to a predetermined pattern is not a virtue; it is a threat to the social fabric woven by decades of behaviorist thinking.

Concerning the transition taking place in current thought, Jim Leffel wrote:

> Modernism's focus on the individual birthed Western democracy. Humans, modernists declare, begin as autonomous, self-governed individuals in a sea of other individuals, each self-interested and consequently each a threat to the other. Modernist political theorists argue that from the primal "state of nature" people come together—for reasons of individual self-interest. They agree to voluntarily limit freedom for the sake of protection. They assume that a person is first an individual, and becomes a social

being by choice. Society exists as the creation of individuals, and its ongoing existence is dependent on the consent of individuals, not vice versa.

Liberal democracy holds water only if humans are free to select between alternative actions. Postmodern theorists, however, reject the idea that people freely reason and choose. Human thought, in their view, can't exist independent of our social environment.[10]

We have already seen that postmodernism is the logical outcome of both Gnosticism and Existentialism. Now we see that it is also the logical outcome of Behaviorism. Postmodernism is the merging of these three philosophies.

Maslow and other behaviorists are not totally wrong in their assessment of human behavior. Nor are the postmodernists who are building upon and transforming the landscape of Behaviorism. Remember that all they are doing is observing human behavior and drawing certain conclusions. What is faulty with their conclusions is not the habitual nature of human behavior but the correlation between cause and effect. What they view as cause may not be the cause at all. Most psychological studies are merely fallen man observing the behavior of fallen man. The greatest danger from Behaviorism as a philosophy is that it removes personal responsibility from human behavior.

Winners and Losers

In the game of "The devil made me do it," there are really no winners; there are only losers. Society in general is the loser, because society needs to be populated by responsible people. Responsibility is necessary for society to function properly. When we drive down the highway, we need to be able to expect that the other car coming toward us is driven by a responsible person who is concerned not only for his own survival but also for the good of others driving on the same highway.

As Behaviorism continues to spread throughout society, throwing a blanket of protection and excuses over more and more antisocial behavior, society continues to breakdown. More and more types of behavior are classified as the result of genetics or illnesses or simply acceptable alternative lifestyles. Addiction itself is viewed as the product of environmental factors, rather than the product of irresponsible choices.

As individuals are led to believe that they cannot help being addicted to certain types of behavior, excusing their behavior leaves them more addicted. The will to choose to act responsibly is lost, which results in further addictive behavior. This increase in addictive behavior is viewed by behaviorists as vindication of their conclusions. However, they ignore the possibility that dissemination of their philosophy may be a major cause for the increase in addictive behavior.

It is no wonder that the postmodernists now preach that people are the product of their culture and only imagine they are self-governing. It is the logical conclusion drawn from decades of trying to manipulate human behavior. More and more antisocial behavior is the product of psychological conditioning. Whole generations have been taught to believe that they have no power over their own behavior and that yielding to the forces of Behaviorism is the way to happiness and fulfillment.

As with philosophies regarding knowledge and existence, Christians are implicated in the fallout from the false philosophy called Behaviorism. The implication comes in two forms. First, Christians are implicated because many have denied the validity of psychology as a discipline and a resource for evaluating behavioral problems in society. Simply recognizing certain behavior patterns does not make one a behaviorist. We need to know what types of behavior are addictive and how to avoid them. By castigating all psychological studies and thereby denying the validity of their findings, many Christians have left themselves open to the manipulations of behaviorists.

Second, Christians are implicated because too little thought has been given to biblical solutions to the various phenomena affecting humans identified by psychologists who have studied behavior. Rather than spending so much effort refuting what is irrefutable, Christians should be taught how to help individuals avoid behavior that is addictive and to break cycles of addiction already established.

Many Christians are frustrated with their own powerlessness to overcome the seductive influences in their lives, or they have given up altogether and actively promote the doctrines of Behaviorism. Many churches use Behaviorism to sell their wares. There is an attitude of "anything goes" in some parts of Christendom. As long as it packs the pews or brings a return on their investment, it is acceptable. If it works, do it.

The flip side is the belief that we must not do anything that might offend those who come to the church already preconditioned by cultural behaviorism. Tell them what they want to hear. Give them what they have been conditioned to expect. It has to be loud, fast, and psychedelic because this generation has been conditioned to be loud, fast, and psychedelic. If it isn't entertaining, they won't buy it. Never suggest that a pattern of behavior might not be pleasing to the Lord nor edifying to the church. Even worse, ignore the truth that what is being done in the church might in fact be addictive and not the fruit of the Holy Spirit.

REFUSING TO PLAY THE GAME: "THE DEVIL MADE ME DO IT"

The Bible warns against yielding to the allurement of this world and failing to exercise personal discipline. Paul exhorts the church to not follow the behavior pattern of the world:

> This I say therefore, and affirm together with the Lord, that you walk no longer just as the Gentiles also walk, in the futility of their mind, being darkened in their understanding, excluded from the life of God, because of the ignorance that is in them, because of the hardness of their heart; and they, having become callous, have given themselves over to sensuality, for the practice of every kind of impurity with greediness. (Ephesians 4:17–19)

This is not a very flattering picture of the world. The picture painted by many behaviorists and postmodernists is not very flattering either and is not unlike the biblical picture. The view that men can be addicted to certain behavior is not new or limited to behaviorists. Paul referred to the problem, "All things are lawful for me, but not all things are profitable. All things are lawful for me, but I will not be *mastered* by anything" (1 Corinthians 6:12, italics mine).

Simply because the law of the land or social mores permit certain behavior does not mean that the behavior is wise. Some behavior is not beneficial, and some behavior can be addictive. Paul took it a step further when he wrote, "Or do you not know that your body is a temple of the Holy Spirit who is in you, whom you have from God, and that you are not your own? For you have been bought with a price: therefore glorify God in your body (1 Corinthians 6:19–20). Christians have been given the freedom through Christ to overcome addictive behavior as well as the responsibility to do so. More than that, we must think about what behavior is consistent with our profession of faith and what behavior is not. We are to be servants of Christ rather than servants of our fleshly appetites.

Paul expressed that same concept another way:

> Therefore do not let sin reign in your mortal body that you should obey its lusts, and do not go on presenting the members of your body to sin [as] instruments of unrighteousness; but present yourselves to

God as those alive from the dead, and your members [as] instruments of righteousness to God. For sin shall not be master over you, for you are not under law but under grace. What then? Shall we sin because we are not under law but under grace? May it never be! Do you not know that when you present yourselves to someone [as] slaves for obedience, you are slaves of the one whom you obey, either of sin resulting in death, or of obedience resulting in righteousness? (Romans 6:12–16)

In another context he wrote:

Brethren, join in following my example, and observe those who walk according to the pattern you have in us. For many walk, of whom I often told you, and now tell you even weeping, [that they are] enemies of the cross of Christ, whose end is destruction, whose god is [their] appetite, and [whose] glory is in their shame, who set their minds on earthly things. (Philippians 3:17–19)

What the behaviorist identifies as addictive behavior, Paul identified as slavery to sin. The only difference is that the behaviorist excludes God and moral absolutes from his frame of reference. By excluding God, he excludes the power that God provides for overcoming harmful behavior. By excluding moral absolutes, he leaves the door open for individuals to engage in behavior that has been judged to be acceptable by men but leads to further addiction.

This section is titled "The Devil Made Me Do It" because Behaviorism as a philosophy removes personal responsibility and encourages finding a scapegoat. It separates behavior from the moral foundation laid down in the Bible. The behaviorists and the society they have created through environmental manipulation determine what is acceptable or unacceptable behavior. Since people are merely cogs in a machine, and good and bad behavior is determined by culture, then, when things go wrong, like the shooting at Columbine High, there are many ready scapegoats. Any thought that it might be the false philosophies of Gnosticism, Existentialism, and Behaviorism as they join together to form a godless, amoral, addictive worldview is out of the question.

Christians must not remain ignorant or indifferent to the influences of Behaviorism. Christian parents need to be better informed concerning the philosophy of Behaviorism in order to help their children avoid its pitfalls. We must understand how addictive behavior patterns are developed. An addiction has both physiological and spiritual elements. Behavioral psychology as a disciplined study of human behavior can assist us in our understanding of the physiological part of the problem.

When behavioral psychology becomes an all-encompassing philosophy that treats man as no more than an animal, and when it denies any moral responsibility on the part of the individual, then it becomes part of the problem and not part of the solution. Behavioral psychology cannot provide what is needed to correct the moral and spiritual parts of addiction. Until the moral and spiritual aspects are resolved, manipulation of the environment may provide short-term improvements. Only a change of the will of the individual will bring lasting change.

Temptation and Behaviorism

As we have already seen, the Bible clearly teaches that environmental factors do play a role in human behavior, even to the point of enslaving a person to certain patterns of behavior. However, instead of trying to find a cause outside of the person—the devil made me do it—the Bible tells us to look inside the person.

James wrote:

> Let no one say when he is tempted, "I am being tempted by God"; for God cannot be tempted by evil, and He Himself does not tempt anyone. But each one is tempted when he is carried away and enticed by his own lust. Then when lust has conceived, it gives birth to sin; and when sin is accomplished, it brings forth death. (James 1:13–15)

Human behavior is not merely a response to factors in the environment. Human behavior begins as an inner impulse directed by the soul, the inner person that is undetectable by scientific methods. The soul of man, as we understand it in this context, refers to the driving force that is only visible through the outward behavior patterns the inner force produces. In Hebrews 4:12, this force is called "the thoughts and intentions of the heart."

Behaviorists deny the existence of the inner force. Yet it is the most important part of man and the part that needs to be changed so that the person is set free from addiction to environmental influences.

Concerning this inner force we read,

> For the word of God is living and active and sharper than any two-edged sword, and piercing as far as the division of soul and spirit, of both joints and marrow, and able to judge *the thoughts and intentions of the heart.* (Hebrews 4:12, italics mine)

By denying the existence of the biblical concept of soul and replacing it with a false concept, the behaviorist makes two serious mistakes. First, he denies the true reality of the soul revealed in the Scriptures. Second, he disavows the very force that can deliver the soul from its bondage to environmental factors that are harmful to society.

The picture that James presents in James 1:13–15, is very clear in the Greek language. The phrase "carried away and enticed" translates a Greek word taken from the fishing industry in James' day. It describes the act of setting out a net in which fish are entrapped. The net is then pulled shut and the fish are drawn into the boat.

This is much like the purse-seine boat today. This valuable illustration helps us understand human behavior and its propensity to do what should not be done. When fishing with a purse-seine boat, the net is laid out in a circle, with the top of the net held on the surface of the water by floats and the bottom of the net pulled deep by heavy weights. As the circle forms, the net acts like a purse that can be drawn together at both the top and bottom. Any living creature in the water encompassed by the net is trapped. When the net is pulled back aboard the seiner, the fish are dragged into the boat.

What takes us many words to explain, James explains in a few. Human behavior is like a purse-seine net. In essence, we set out nets by which we entrap ourselves. The net is made up of the little desires that seem insignificant by themselves. When the net is deployed and the purse is pulled tight, we are trapped by the bigger sin we would not otherwise have committed.

The truth of the illustration was underscored several years ago when I was the pastor of a church near the ocean. One of the members of the church was the wife of a purse-seine fisherman. One day, she asked me why she seemed to continue to commit the same sin over and over again, even though she prayed hard and worked hard to avoid it. I referred her to what James wrote in James 1:13–15 and illustrated it by asking her to recall the way her husband caught fish. I suggested that she examine the pattern of behavior leading up to the sin she was trying to avoid. What decisions did she make and what desires did she satisfy that, when strung together, might form a trap like a purse-seine net? I counseled her that once she identified the decisions that formed the net entrapping her and stopped that pattern of behavior, she would be able to overcome the bigger sin.

A few weeks later, that woman reported, "Pastor, it's working." She was able to identify the trap she had set for herself that for years had caused her downfall. She was finally able to overcome the big sin.

Every Christian needs to recognize the truth of this passage in James. The behaviorist is not wrong when he sees a propensity to addictive behavior. Not all of us have the same propensities, but we all have propensities. The author of the Book of Hebrews refers to them as "sin which so easily entangles us" (Hebrews 12:1). A sin that entangles one person may not entangle another. We need to identify what it is that entangles us and get it out of our lives. It is even more critical to do this today because there are many more enticements because of Bahaviorism.

Behaviorism is not the innocuous boon to society it is purported to be. In fact, it has become a major cause of the problem. It places more and more stumbling blocks in our way than at any time in human history. Those stumbling blocks are made possible by the conclusions drawn from behavioral psychology and used to produce and market addictive behavior. Parents need to guide their children into a better understanding of the danger of addictive behavior, including those addictions made possible through the wiles of behavioral psychology. Such things as video games and other repetitive activities are very addictive. Those who produce the products know this but sell them anyway. A behavior does not have to be violent or sexually explicit to be harmful. Whenever we allow a repetitive behavior to control us, we have ceased to be controlled by the One who has every right to control us, the Lord Jesus Christ.

Submitting to the Lordship of Christ
Overcomes Behaviorism

The best way to insure that we are not victims of Behaviorism is to make sure we acknowledge Christ as Lord over every aspect of life. It is important to understand that we do not *make* Him Lord. He is Lord. His death on the cross gave Him the sole right to the title along with all of the authority and power. Our task is to acknowledge His lordship by choosing to do what pleases Him. To do otherwise is to leave ourselves open to the enslaving power of the world around us. Paul wrote: "But thanks be to God that though you were slaves of sin, you became obedient from the heart to that form of teaching to which you were committed" (Romans 6:17).

A serious error parents make is to attempt to force their children into a pattern of behavior through authoritarian tactics. Authoritarianism is the use of laws to control human behavior. In doing so, they ignore the inner force of the soul. The outcome is the same as when behaviorists deny this inner force. It amounts to trying to change behavior without a corresponding change in the inner force. Authoritarianism is no more effective in controlling behavior than when behaviorists set out to control a child by manipulating the environment. Paul noted that sinful passions are aroused by the Law (Romans 7:5). Therefore, resorting to authoritarianism to modify behavior will usually result in further harmful behavior.

It is true that a young child needs a structured environment in which to grow up. However, parents will not always be able to control that environment. After children reach an age where they are able to reason for themselves, trying to control them via authority only causes them to rebel. Instead, children need to be taught how to walk in the Spirit by voluntarily yielding their will to the control of the Holy Spirit.

This does not mean that we abandon our attempts to provide a structured environment in the home. A well-organized home includes a structured environment. There are times when we go to bed and times when we get up. There are times when we play, and there are times when we work. We all have responsibilities we must fulfill in life. Teaching responsibility is not the same as authoritarian control.

Authoritarian control is what parents do when they fail to take into account the will of the child. Remember that raising a child is a partnership between the parent and the child. Unfortunately, too many parents try to do it alone, without the child's cooperation. That cooperation must be secured early, before harmful or addictive behavior patterns are developed. There are many ways to achieve cooperation. Ultimately, it is achieved by teaching the child how to walk in the Spirit (Cf. Galatians 5:16–24, Ephesians 5:18). Walking in the Spirit is a choice we make when we decide to do what is right in God's eyes, rather than follow our own inner impulses. We will talk more about the act of choosing to do what is right in the chapter on love.

The best way to partnership with our children is to practice biblical principles ourselves. Then we must allow them the freedom to do it on their own. This does not mean we allow them to do something that would be very harmful to them. We are still responsible to protect them and nurture them. Once the child understands the lordship of Christ, we must not place ourselves in the position of lord or master in that child's life. Doing so robs them of the opportunity to learn how to submit to their true Lord, the Lord Jesus Christ.

In many respects, Paul was a spiritual parent to the churches at Corinth and at Philippi. The comparison of two texts explains a valuable truth for us to follow when seeking to guide others to submit to the lordship of Christ. The first is found in 2 Corinthians 1:23–24. Paul wrote, "But I call God as witness to my soul, that to spare you I did not come again to Corinth. Not that we lord it over your faith, but are workers with you for your joy; for in your faith you are standing firm."

When Paul wrote this letter to the Corinthian church, he was teaching in the school of Tyrannus in Ephesus many miles away (Acts 19:9). He had planned to visit the Corinthian church on one of his travels, but when he heard about some problems at Corinth, he changed his travel plans and did not go there. His reason for the change in plans was that he did not want to lord it over the Christians in Corinth by going there personally. He sent a letter instead. He wanted their correct response to be to the lordship of Christ, not to Paul's physical presence. Here we can see an important principle about how to teach others to respond to the lordship of Christ. We must not hover over them every minute to make sure that they do exactly what we want them to do. Again, the amount of involvement needed to raise children depends upon their age and how well they respond to the lordship of Christ in their lives.

The second passage where we find principles taught regarding the lordship of Christ is in Philippians 2:12–13. Paul was in prison in Rome. He heard of some problems in the church in Philippi in Macedonia but could not go to Philippi personally to ensure that the problems were corrected. He wrote:

> So then, my beloved, just as you have always obeyed, not as in my presence only, but now much more in my absence, work out your salvation with fear and trembling; for it is God who is at work in you, both to will and to work for [His] good pleasure.

Paul used a play on words in the Greek language to explain an important principle regarding the lordship of Christ. The play on words is formed by two words. The first is *parousia* and the second is *apousia*. *Parousia* is translated as "presence," and the second, *apousia*, is translated "absence." *Parousia* refers to the effect one's personal presence has upon the behavior of others when present. This important word is used several times regarding the future return of the Lord Jesus Christ. Since His return is in the future, it is translated as "coming." However, the force of the word is the effect His presence will have upon human behavior at His coming.

This meaning is very clear when Paul wrote about his own presence in another context. Individuals had accused him of duplicity in behaving one way when present and another way when absent. He wrote, "For they say, 'His letters are weighty and strong, but his personal *presence* is unimpressive and his speech contemptible'" (2 Corinthians 10:10, italics mine).

The important principle from the Philippian passage is that those of us who are parents need to discipline our children in a manner that recognizes the presence of God in their lives. We need to be very careful not to interject ourselves into their lives in such a way that they never learn how to depend upon the presence of God. Authoritarian parenting amounts to lording it over our children. It is detrimental to the spiritual development of children because, when the parents are no longer around, they will not know how to rely upon Christ's lordship in their lives.

When our daughter, Tamara, was six years of age, we moved into a new neighborhood. There was another girl her age living in the neighborhood whose parents were not providing any guidance at all. On Saturday mornings they would kick the little girl out of the house and lock the door so she could not get back in. Many times, we would find her wandering around the neighborhood without proper clothing and without breakfast.

One winter day when I was working in the backyard, Tamara and the little girl came around to where I was working. I noticed Tamara did not have her coat on, and I asked her to put it on because it was cold. She replied that her friend did not have a coat on and so she did not want to wear hers either. I asked her, "Are you going to do what you want to do, or are you going to do what is right?"

She answered, "What is right." With that, the two girls disappeared around the house to play in another part of the yard out of my sight. I began to wonder if Tamara had actually put her coat on, and I peeked around the corner of the house to see. She was wearing her coat and the matter was closed. All she needed me to do was remind her what was the right thing to do, and she did it without being coerced.

We are not successful parents when we are able to force our children to do what we want them to do by our presence. We are successful when our children learn to do what is right even when we are not present. By beginning early, children who are truly born again will readily respond to the leading of the Holy Spirit in their lives and acknowledge Christ's lordship over them. This does not mean they will be sinless little angels. They will still make mistakes, but we, as adults, do too.

If we are to avoid playing "The devil made me do it," we must lead our children to Jesus Christ first as their savior. Then we need to help them develop the concept of Christ's lordship in their lives. This is the only defense against the influence of Behaviorism that is permeating society today.

PART III

A BETTER WAY

CHAPTER SIX

Concepts of Love that Do Not Build Relationships

The problems in society could be solved if individuals would truthfully fulfill their God-given responsibilities in every relationship, whether they are relationships of circumstance, purpose, or fulfillment. In order to do this, each individual needs to learn how to communicate effectively. The basic message we need to communicate in order to strengthen our relationships is a concern for others and a desire to meet their needs, sometimes even before our own. We must put *responsibility* back into the meaning of relationship. We need to fulfill our responsibilities and be assured that others in the relationship will fulfill theirs.

There are some popular philosophies that work against and even destroy healthy relationships, preventing effective communication from taking place. These philosophies—philosophies regarding knowledge, existence, and behavior—work against us by breaking down the fabric of society necessary for building relationships.

The problems in the world today are so vast and complex that no simple bromide or pat answer is going to resolve them. However, the answer is simpler than one might expect. It is as simple as the lyrics to a popular song a few years ago: "What the world needs now is love sweet love." Unfortunately, what the songwriter had in mind is not what the Bible calls love.

The love of the world is based upon the philosophies of Gnosticism, Existentialism, and Behaviorism. These philosophies have a common denominator. They are based on human reasoning and self-gratification. They exclude God and the supernatural. They excuse irresponsible behavior and relieve mankind of the duty to accept responsibilities in relationships.

For love to overcome the destructive forces of such philosophies, it must begin with and become an extension of the work of God in our lives. This is exactly what biblical love does. But before we can define biblical love, we need to identify what it is not. Any love based upon human philosophies, like the philosophies themselves, is destructive.

SEX IS NOT LOVE

Before we can clearly define biblical love, we must recognize what it is not. Biblical love is not sex. Much of what we see and hear in the world today contradicts this one simple statement. Sex is viewed as the greatest experience in life. Freudian psychology viewed love as the foundation of human relationships. Behavioral psychology reinforced that concept by placing sex in the hierarchy of needs as a prepotent need that must be satisfied before most of the other needs can be satisfied.

The Bible Never Refers to Sex as Love

Nowhere in the Bible is love ever described as sex. Of course, the English term for sex is not found in the Bible. The closest word is found in Hebrews 13:4, where we read, "Marriage [is to be held] in honor among all, and the [marriage] bed [is to be] undefiled; for fornicators and adulterers God will judge." The Greek term translated "[marriage] bed" is *koite,* from which comes the English word *coitus,* meaning sexual intercourse. In the four contexts in which the Greek term is found, three clearly refer to engaging in sexual intercourse. In the Hebrew passage, we are exhorted to honor intercourse and are warned that fornication and adultery dishonor it and will bring God's judgment.

In the Old Testament, the Hebrew word that most approximates the English word for sex is *yada,* which is translated by some English versions "to know." However, in the 1,040 occurrences of *yada* in the Old Testament, the King James Version never translates *yada* "love."

In some English translations, there are a few Old Testament passages where other Hebrew terms are translated "love" and where the reference made in the context approximates the physical relationship. But in almost every one of those contexts, there are destructive forces at work in the relationship.

Consider the love Amnon had for Tamar in 2 Samuel 13. The context makes it clear that it was not a healthy kind of love. In fact, after forcing his half-sister to lay with him, we read, "Then Amnon hated her with a very great hatred; for the hatred with which he hated her was greater than the love with which he had loved her. And Amnon said to her, 'Get up, go away!'" (2 Samuel 13:15). Amnon's actions from beginning to end were the very opposite of biblical love. Yet they describe the love of the world, which is a logical extension of the erroneous philosophies regarding knowledge, existence, and behavior.

Amnon's treatment of Tamar is probably the best example in the Bible of the sexual self-gratification so often viewed today as love for several reasons. To begin with, Tamar was his half-sister. His love was a forbidden love. While marriage in such a relationship was not unheard of in those days, the Law of Moses forbids marriage between blood relatives (Compare Leviticus 18:6–17).

The second thing we see about Amnon's act is that he was unconcerned for the welfare of Tamar. Tamar expressed a willingness to marry Amnon if forced into it. However, it was not her desire to do so. Tamar was coerced into having sex. The tragedy of viewing love as sex is that love is then defined by the passion of the moment, without any regard for what is best for both of the partners. This is conquest, not love. Where there is conquest, there is competition. With competition, there are winners and losers. Historically, the losers have been women. While conquest is more consistent with the makeup of men than of women, in some cultures—including the present culture in America—some women adopt the concept of conquest even though it is not naturally a part of their makeup. In the account of Amnon, Amnon was the winner and Tamar was clearly the loser.

A third lesson is that Amnon's treatment of Tamar was the result of passion, the opposite of biblical love. There was no consideration of personal responsibility on his part. Once his sexual appetite was assuaged, his passion turned to hate. This is the best argument against defining love as sex. Sooner or later, the passion is gone, and because there was no genuine love from the beginning, sexual passion is then replaced by some other form of self-gratification.

Finally, we see that Amnon's actions sowed seeds of turmoil in his family that bore bitter fruit for years. It eventually led to Amnon's murder. Amnon's actions, in reality, turned into self-hate because it damaged every other relationship in Amnon's life. The unfolding of events from that fateful moment demonstrates the truth that we reap what we sow (Galatians 6:7–8). More than any other truth about sex, the fact that we reap what we sow needs to be taught to children before they engage in promiscuous sex.

In most Old Testament passages where love is associated with sex, the context describes either harlotry or spiritual adultery and, therefore, a perversion of the relationship. Harlotry is the epitome of self-gratification because personal responsibility and self-control are excluded. Spiritual adultery is the act of giving to a false god the love that God alone deserves. Throughout human history, we find harlotry associated with spiritual adultery. The same is true today. Many aberrant forms of Christianity eventually degenerate into some form of sexual deviation.

In other passages where commentators find love associated with sex, the association must be supplied through the English word *love,* because it is not automatically derived from the Hebrew terms. The same is true in the Greek New Testament. When we stop to consider the matter, sex should not automatically be associated with *love* and needs to be expressed or implied by the context in which the word is found. Because of the false philosophies prevalent in society, the context of love is often assumed to be associated with sex. One of the dilemmas of Western culture is how to disassociate sex from love so that positive expressions of genuine love can be experienced apart from sex.

It is the association of love with sex that is the most disturbing and damaging concept in the three basic philosophies that we have looked at so far. In the dualistic world of the Gnostic, there is a distorted view of the physical world. The view that the physical union between a man and a woman is immoral, dirty, or degrading stems from the Gnostic view that the physical world is evil. Eventually, this form of Gnosticism leads to *asceticism,* which is the denial of normal physical appetites. The other extreme holds that, since the physical world is evil and earthly and not part of the spiritual world, the physical appetites can be indulged to the fullest. That form of Gnosticism leads to every form of debauchery. *Hedonism,* the philosophy that what brings the greatest pleasure is the greatest good, is a form of this type of Gnosticism.

In the world of Existentialism, the individual is encouraged to define his or her own existence any way that pleases him or her. If it includes behavior that the Bible classifies as sin, then the solution is to get rid of the Bible. The individual is the final arbiter of what is right and wrong. Because Existentialism sees individuals alienated from each other in a hostile and absurd world, it does not lend itself to loving others but, instead, accentuates self-love.

For the behaviorist, the individual is defined as merely a creature with physical appetites susceptible to the enticements of the environment. Since there are no moral absolutes, any behavior viewed by society as appropriate is acceptable as long as it does not interfere with the rights of others to follow their own basic instincts.

Is any of this new? Absolutely not. In fact, these very philosophies merely rehash what the Bible already said about man's rejection of God and what God has revealed about Himself.

> Therefore God gave them over in the lusts of their hearts to impurity, that their bodies might be dishonored among them. For they exchanged the truth of God for a lie, and worshipped and served the creature rather than the Creator, who is blessed forever. Amen. For this reason God gave them over to degrading passions; for their women exchanged the natural function for that which is unnatural, and in

the same way also the men abandoned the natural
function of the woman and burned in their desire
toward one another, men with men committing in-
decent acts and receiving in their own persons the
due penalty of their error. (Romans 1:24–27)

Damage to physical relationships between humans
was the first noticeable effect of the Fall, when sin entered the world. Therefore, it is not hard to understand
that sexual behavior is where redemption must begin.
It cannot begin as long as we hold onto the false philosophies stemming from the Fall. We must be restored
in our minds so that we overcome Gnosticism. We must
be restored in our relationships so that we overcome
Existentialism. We must be restored in our behavior so
that we overcome Behaviorism. A clear understanding
of biblical love will do that for us if we allow this understanding to shape our lives.

Sex Should Be an Expression of Obedience

Our worldview must include the restoration of the
concept of absolute truth. Any form of Gnosticism must
be rejected. We must allow the absolute truth of God to
sit in judgment upon our subjective, experiential truth
and change our minds so that our worldview coincides
with God's worldview. Next, we need to acknowledge
the reality of existence as defined by God. We must reject
Existentialism and give up the thought that we can create our own existence apart from God. Finally, we must
accept our God-given responsibilities in our relationships

with others. This means we must reject Behaviorism as a philosophy. Instead of seeing life as a process that leads from one level of self-gratification and fulfillment in life to merely greater self-gratification, we need to see that fulfillment in life comes when we put others first in our relationships and ourselves second. Genuine fulfillment in life is achieved by meeting the needs of others.

Sex, as it was intended by God, was first and foremost an act of obedience to God. God commanded Adam and Eve to be fruitful and multiply (Genesis 1:28). It was a responsibility that carried restrictions and limitations from the beginning. Adam was to cleave to his wife, and the two were to be one flesh. That excluded sex from all other relationships. While gratification is involved, it is not self-gratification. It is the satisfaction of meeting the needs of one's marriage partner. That is why Paul instructs both the husband and the wife to perform his or her duty to the marriage partner (1 Corinthians 7:3).

God meets our needs through others and, in turn, wants to use us to meet the needs of others. Accepting our responsibility to meet the needs of others requires that we put the needs of others in any relationship ahead of our own. In the matter of sex, it means that we will not engage in destructive behavior that will ultimately prevent us from meeting the needs of one another, such as engaging in promiscuous sex outside of marriage.

Sex, when performed within the boundaries that God has set, can be one of the most fulfilling experiences in life. This fulfillment comes as we meet the needs of each other in a God-honoring relationship. Sometimes fulfillment is achieved by denying ourselves in order to meet the needs of others. By enabling us to meet our responsibilities in every relationship, biblical love demonstrates in practice that the philosophies of Gnosticism, Existentialism, and Behaviorism are false.

We need to educate our children regarding God's intended plan for sex. We need to teach our children that sex is not for self-gratification. We need to reclaim sex as an expression of our obedience to God and demonstrate this obedience to our children by our attitudes and our actions. We need to help our children tune out the destructive forces of the false philosophies of Gnosticism, Existentialism, and Behaviorism, which promote rapacious sex. We need to help our children develop their sexuality in a way that glorifies our Creator.

There are five Greek words that are often associated with love in the New Testament. They are *storge, epithumia, eros, agape,* and *philia.* Only two of these, *agape* and *philia,* are translated "love" in the New Testament. We will discover the meaning of these two words and their relationship to each other in the next chapter. First we need to consider *storge, epithumia,* and *eros,* which are not suitable to be translated "love" because of their root meanings in the Greek language.

STORGE: NATURAL AFFECTION

Storge refers to natural affection and is used only twice in the New Testament. Both times it is used in the negative, *astorge* (*a* renders it negative in Greek), and is translated "without natural affection" (Romans 1:31, 2 Timothy

3:3). It is used once in combination with *philia* and translated in the King James Version as "kindly affectionate" (Romans 12:10). It is never translated "love."

C. S. Lewis put this word into perspective when he wrote:

> Affection would not be affection if it was loudly and frequently expressed; to produce it in public is like getting your household furniture out for a move. It did very well in its place, but it looks shabby or tawdry or grotesque in the sunshine. Affection almost slinks or seeps through our lives. It lives with humble, un-dress, private things; soft slippers, old clothes, old jokes, the thump of a sleepy dog's tail on the kitchen floor, the sound of a sewing-machine, a gollywog left on the lawn.[1]

Leon Morris wrote this regarding *storge*:

> It is all the more interesting that the term is never used in the New Testament. Coming closest to it is the negative form of the corresponding adjective, which indicates disapproval. Twice people "without natural affection" are condemned (Rom. 1:31; II Tim. 3:3). There can be no doubt from the general thrust of New Testament teaching, and specifically from what it has to say about the family, that the early Christians saw *storge* as natural and right. But their failure to use the word in the New Testament documents shows that it was not *storge* that they had in mind when they spoke of love.[2]

Consistency, familiarity, and expectancy, all connotations of the Greek word storge, can be positives in a relationship. By themselves and without other virtues they can destroy a relationship. A husband can expect his wife to wait on him hand and foot. Upheavals in a relationship due to changing circumstances can cause *storge* to evaporate. Any form of addiction destroys natural affection by focusing attention upon self-gratification. The prevalent picture of codependency is *storge* taken to an extreme. This is perhaps why the Holy Spirit never uses the term in a context that demands a higher word for love.

Storge is not an adequate concept for love because of the damage done to it by the threefold philosophies of Gnosticism, Existentialism, and Behaviorism. As we have seen, these philosophies do not encourage relationships; they destroy them. Since *storge* depends upon relationships for its existence and adds little to those relationships, it is easily destroyed.

Gnosticism promotes selfishness based upon personal knowledge. It encourages the one who acquired the knowledge to see himself above others. Paul wrote, "knowledge makes arrogant, but love edifies" (1 Corinthians 8:1). Those who don't know sense the condescension of those who claim to know. As Gnosticism is lived out in the real world, it evolves into intimidation, and eventually tyranny, as those who know lord it over those who don't know. *Storge*—natural affection—cannot overcome, let alone survive, such feelings of superiority and inferiority. Any true love must overcome those destructive forces in any relationship.

Existentialism destroys *storge* because it is based upon a sense of alienation that is foreign to *storge*. The attempt to define self-existence separates us from others around us, and the desire to be different stifles any sense of belonging. As this philosophy is lived out, individuals begin to relate to each other through their differences rather than through a common identity. Diversity is the focus, and it becomes the all-important commonality. *Storge* cannot exist when the primary focus is diversity, because it is the opposite of diversity.

This does not mean that there cannot be unity in diversity. There can and must be in order for society to function at all. However, the diversity of Existentialism exists, not because of circumstances but because of a contrived difference that stems from a rebellion against the majority and a denial of natural, God-given commonality. Existential diversity is the driving force of the political-correctness of postmodernism, not a genuine appreciation for inherent diversity.

For *storge* to exist, individuals must be allowed to form natural bonds in given circumstances. Those bonds should not be viewed as a threat to other groups who have also formed natural bonds. *Storge* is simply natural affection stemming from a commonality. Destroy that common identity for any reason and *storge* is destroyed.

Storge has no power to build bonds where chasms exist, but biblical love can bridge chasms between diverse groups and enable those groups to work together in spite of their diversity. The ideal would be to transform individuals, and thereby to give them a new identity. That would be the easiest way for *storge* to flourish.

In fact, this is what happens when we are genuinely born again and enter the family of God. Paul wrote:

> For you are all sons of God through faith in Christ Jesus. For all of you who were baptized into Christ have clothed yourselves with Christ. There is neither Jew nor Greek, there is neither slave nor free man, there is neither male nor female; for you are all one in Christ Jesus. (Galatians 3:26–28)

Behaviorism promotes a lifestyle of selfishness because individuals are conditioned to respond to the environment mindlessly. Self-gratification is seen as the driving force of life, rather than a desire to reach out to others and to support and build others up. Because Behaviorism is based upon a hierarchy of self-gratification and the theory that one will not be motivated to move to the higher level of gratification until the lower needs are satisfied, the goal of building relationships—fulfilling the needs of others—is difficult because it is a low priority on the scale of hierarchical needs. As long as the individual's self-gratification at the lower level has not been met, there is little motivation to move to the higher levels. Because physical appetites tend to grow when there is no willful attempt to curb them, the needs identified as prepotent require more and more effort to be assuaged, thus delaying any upward movement on the scale.

Behaviorism is a potent force in society today, a force that storge is unable to overcome. To be effective, biblical love must overcome the preconditioning of each of the three categories of philosophies: Gnosticism, Existentialism, and Behaviorism. It does so perfectly as we will see in Chapter 7.

EPITHUMIA: DESIRE, PASSION, LUST

Another word group often associated with love is *epithumia* (the noun) and *epithumeo* (the verb). It is found frequently in the New Testament.[3] This is the first of a list of five Greek words discussed by Dr. Ed Wheat, M.D., in a taped message he titled "Love Life for Every Married Couple."

> When it is used in the Bible in a negative way it is translated "lust." When it is used in a positive way it is translated "desire" and this is the way we will be using the word. For in your marriage you and your mate should have a strong physical sexual desire for each other. You may not have this at the present time simply because other aspects of your relationship are not working as they should.[4]

We need to carefully compare Dr. Wheat's teaching in this taped series with the teaching of the New Testament. Of the fifty-nine times *epithmia* and its cognates are used in the New Testament, it is used only eight times as positive desire. It is never used positively with the physical appetites of the body.[5] It is curious that Dr. Wheat begins by defining that term as something to be promoted. He calls it "love" even while admitting that it is never referred to as such in the New Testament.

A background of the word will help us to better understand the issues. *Epithumia* comes from two Greek words: the preposition *epi*, translated "upon"; and *thumos*, translated "passion."[6] "Thumos . . . fundamentally denotes violent movement."[7] To that is added, "From the sense of to well up, to boil up . . ."[8] A further comparison of the use of this word will give an overall picture of why the New Testament does not use it either for love or for the sexual relationship legitimately expressed in marriage.

> In Greek philosophy, *epithumia* is the waywardness of man in conflict with his rationality. . . . In the OT and Judaism epithumia is an offence against God, who demands of man total obedience and love from the whole heart, Dt. 5:5.[9]

> In Paul . . . *epithumia* is evil, not because it is irrational, but because it is disobedience to the command of God . . . the essential point in *epithumia* is that it is desire as impulse, as a motion of the will. It is, in fact, lust, since the thought of satisfaction gives pleasure and that of non-satisfaction pain. *Epithumia* is anxious self-seeking. . . . In *epithumia* man is seen as he really is, the more so because *epithumia* bursts upon him with the force of immediacy. Even after the reception of the divine Spirit, *epithumia* is always a danger against which man must be warned and must fight.[10]

Paul equates *epithumia* with the reign of sin in the body and forbids such for the Christian (Romans 6:12).

The believer is to "make no provision for the flesh in regard to its lusts" (Romans 13:14). Paul wrote, "For this is the will of God, your sanctification; [that is], that you abstain from sexual immorality; that each of you know how to possess his own vessel in sanctification and honor" (1 Thessalonians 4:3–4). Concerning this passage, Leon Morris wrote:

> The God-empowered man rules his body. He is not caught in the grip of lustful passions he is quite unable to control. . . . It is a solemn thought that those who reject the knowledge of God which has been afforded them thereby make it inevitable that they will be given over to evil passions.[11]

Therefore, *epithumia*, as the word is used in the New Testament, should not be used as a positive synonym for love. When used of negative passion, it is passion that pulls one down and away from God. One last quote will help to settle the issue. Paul, in his testimony in Romans 7, wrote:

> What shall we say then? Is the Law sin? May it never be! On the contrary, I would not have come to know sin except through the Law; for I would not have known about coveting [*epithumian*] if the Law had not said, "YOU SHALL NOT COVET [*epithumesies*]." But sin, taking opportunity through the commandment, produced in me coveting [*epithumian*] of every kind; for apart from the Law sin [is] dead." (Romans 7:7–8)

Note that the Law Paul quoted was taken from the Old Testament Law commonly referred to as the Ten Commandments. Paul does not state what it was that he coveted. However, it is clear from the passage that the basic meaning of the word refers to an overwhelming desire to have something one does not already possess or to have more of it. Since not coveting is a command, we have the ability to choose not to express *epithumia*. God requires that we make the right choice or suffer the consequences. Christians are commanded to "walk by the Spirit, and you will not carry out the desire [*epithumian*] of the flesh" (Galatians 5:16).

Epithumia is not limited to sexual desire, though that is its major expression. It is any passion that can conquer and destroy the life of a believer who does not learn to control it. It is an insatiable appetite that grows with the feeding of it. The desire does not need to be sexual in nature to be destructive. It is earthy and unredeemable in its natural expression. Notice John's warning:

> Do not love the world, nor the things in the world. If anyone loves the world, the love of the Father is not in him. For all that is in the world, the lust [*epithumia*] of the flesh and the lust [*epithumia*] of the eyes and the boastful pride of life, is not from the Father, but is from the world. And the world is passing away, and [also] its lusts [*epithumia*]; but the one who does the will of God abides forever. (1 John 2:15–17)

This is the type of passion that every Christian needs to avoid. With rare exception, it should not be a part of any relationship. Note the following references to *epithumia* in the New Testament:

> But put on the Lord Jesus Christ, and make no provision for the flesh in regard to [its] lusts. (Romans 13:14)

> But I say, walk by the Spirit, and you will not carry out the desire of the flesh. (Galtaians 5:16)

> Now those who belong to Christ Jesus have crucified the flesh with its passions and desires. (Galatians 5:24)

> . . . that, in reference to your former manner of life, you lay aside the old self, which is being corrupted in accordance with the lusts of deceit, (Ephesians 4:22)

> Therefore consider the members of your earthly body as dead to immorality, impurity, passion, evil desire, and greed, which amounts to idolatry. (Colossians 3:5)

> For the grace of God has appeared, bringing salvation to all men, instructing us to deny ungodliness and worldly desires and to live sensibly, righteously and godly in the present age, (Titus 2:11–12)

Far from counseling couples to cultivate *epithumia*, pastors and counselors should be warning God's people to flee from this destructive emotion. Parents need to teach their children to flee as well. Hollywood and the entertainment industry are not going to tell the truth regarding it, because *epithumia* sells. It is very addictive. But God through Christ can save us from the destructive forces of *epithumia*.

When Christian counselors and sex therapists promote *epithumia* in marriage, they overlook the destructive force of the concept. Because it is self-centered, it promotes self-gratification instead of pleasing one's marriage partner. Because *epithumia* is an overwhelming urge that can lead to addiction, it can become uncontrollable. Addiction of any kind destroys relationships. The goal in the marriage union is mutual fulfillment and satisfaction, not unbridled self-gratification. For this reason, it is important that couples avoid any form of pornography. Not only is pornography an act of adultery committed in the mind (compare Matthew 5:27–28), it also heightens the sexual appetite, making it more difficult to assuage.

We have seen that the three basic philosophies—Gnosticism, Existentialism, and Behaviorism—all destroyed natural affection, *storge*, because *storge* has no power to overcome the forces unleashed by these philosophies. In a sense, the opposite is true of *epithumia*. False concepts of knowledge, existence, and behavior feed *epithumia*, making it stronger and stronger until the individual is powerless to overcome it. The more addictive the behavior, the greater the chance that the individual soul will be overpowered and the life destroyed.

As *epithumia* grows, relationships are destroyed as well. Because *epithumia* is focused on the gratification of the self-life, meeting the needs of others is not the focus. Because of its tendency to overpower the individual, any relationship with others is destroyed. *Epithumia*, more than any other Greek word, matches the compulsiveness behaviorists see in human behavior. *Epithumia*, coupled with the denial of the supernatural in Behaviorism, becomes an uncontrollable force in human behavior. Biblical love must be able to conquer this force.

Eros: Love Without Fulfillment

Before we discuss this third Greek word often associated with love, we need to be reminded that the New Testament never speaks of sex as love. Sex may involve love, and love may involve sex, but the two concepts are not interchangeable. This might be a hard concept to understand given the obsession with sex in society today. There is a constant conditioning taking place whereby each succeeding generation is brought under the influence of a culture steeped in sexual passion and a desire for self-gratification apart from relationships of fulfillment, as if the need to satisfy personal desires is the single driving force in society. Western culture is preoccupied with sex. Sex sells and sex is used to sell everything.

Behaviorism, with its view that the physical appetites, including sex, are the most prepotent motivating forces in life, is culpable in this exploitation of sex. Perhaps the most destructive aspect of the present obsession with sex is that young people are introduced to sex at an earlier age. While I do not have any scientific data to support it, I believe that the trend of children reaching puberty earlier than ever before is because they are being introduced through the media to the emotions associated with sex before they are ready. I believe that it is causing biological changes to take place in children. It is true that, in history, marriage at a young age was acceptable. However, because of the breakdown of the extended family, which once provided support for those who married young, and other social and economic pressures, marriage at a young age is unacceptable in today's culture. Therefore, the sexual revolution is devastating to young people. It teases them into thoughts of promiscuity and enslaves them to desires that cannot be fulfilled biblically.

In history, youthful love is perhaps the best illustration of *eros*. It is love that is forbidden and cannot be assuaged. The behaviorist assumes at the beginning that sexual passion is a basic motivating factor that overrides most other needs. It is considered to be an uncontrollable appetite. Generally what behaviorists see as love is *eros*. This Greek word is probably the best known of the Greek words for love. We find it in the English word *erotic*. The meanings that have been attached to it down through the centuries are about as numerous as the meanings of the English word *love*.

Arndt and Gingrich define *eros* as "passionate love."[12] Stauffer commented:

> *Eros* is a general love of the world seeking satisfaction wherever it can. . . . eros is determined by a

more or less indefinite impulsion toward its object. . . . eran in its highest sense is used of the upward impulsion of man, of his love for the divine. . . . eros seeks in others the fulfillment of its own life's hunger.[13]

Here we see a similarity to *epithumia*. Yet there are important distinctions. *Epithumia*, to the Greek mind, overpowered and pulled men down. *Eros*, on the other hand, did not necessarily pull one down but instead could lift him up.

Anders Nygren, in his monumental work, traced for us Plato's attempt to elevate *eros* to the level of religious love or "'heavenly Eros,' a love for the bright world of ideas, a longing to participate in the Divine life."[14] Dr. Nygren's purpose was to present *eros* and *agape*, another Greek term we will consider in the next chapter, in contrast so that no one would confuse the two regardless of how hard some philosophers might try. He points to the fact that the two stem from two opposing fundamental motifs. Nygren concluded:

> There cannot actually be any doubt that Eros and Agape belong originally to two entirely separate spiritual worlds, between which no direct communication is possible. They do not represent the same value in their respective contexts, so that they cannot in any circumstances be rightly substituted for one another.[15]

Debating with Plato's definition of *eros* as love for God or the divine principle is not our problem today, because *eros* has once again returned to the language of physical passion and pleasure. *Eros* in Greek mythology was the god of love, son of Aphrodite, and identified by the Romans with Cupid, the little imp characterized on Valentine's Day.[16] Plato's monumental effort to change the minds of men was a virtual failure. Men still think of *eros* as sexual pleasure.[17]

Bishop Trench wrote:

> Eros might have fared as so many other words have fared, might have been consecrated anew, despite the deep degradation of its past history; and there were tendencies already working for this in the Platonist use of it, namely, as the longing and yearning desire after that unseen but eternal Beauty, the faint vestiges of which may here be everywhere traced; *ouranios eros*, Philo in this sense has called it. . . . But in the very fact that eros . . . did express this yearning desire . . . this longing after the unpossessed . . . lay its deeper unfitness to set forth that Christian love. . . . [18]

Usually today love is viewed as passion or pleasure. Arthur Colman defines love as "the experience of ecstasy in an interpersonal relationship."[19] A. H. Maslow wrote:

> The core of the description of love must be subjective or phenomenological rather than objective or behavioral. No description, no words can ever communicate the full equality of the love experience to one who has himself never felt it. It consists

primarily of a feeling of tenderness and affection with great enjoyment, happiness, and satisfaction in experiencing this feeling (if all is going well). There is a tendency to want to get closer, to come into more intimate contact, to touch and embrace the loved person, to yearn for him. . . . This feeling of pleasure in contact and in being with, shows itself also in the desire to be together with the loved one as much as possible in as many situations as possible: in work, in play, during esthetic and intellectual pursuits.[20]

James W. Davies took Anders Nygren to task for failing to see *eros* as sexual love when he wrote:

Nowhere in his book does Nygren deal substantially with common eros, that is, with libido. Instead he passes over it, treating it as an unworthy representative of Platonic eros, considering instead the heavenly eros of Plato as being the better match in the contest between eros and agape. He is not unaware of the elements of common eros in the heavenly eros of Platonic philosophy. . . . It is a serious shortcoming of Nygren's presentation that vulgar Eros (as Plato termed what Freud calls the libido) is regarded as unfit for competition with agape because Nygren thereby overlooks what Freud came to discover as a basic drive of the human self. Of course, Nygren would simply write off libido, so-discovered, as egocentric, sensual, and sinful.[21]

By making this judgment of Nygren, Davies demonstrates a flawed understanding of the biblical concept of love expressed by agape which Nygren was trying to present.

Dr. Wheat defined *eros* as that love

> ... which more than any other kind carries with it the idea of romance. It is not always sensual, but it does include the idea of yearning to unite with and the drive to possess the object of one's love. Eros is romantic, passionate and sentimental.[22]

In this statement Wheat ignores the tawdry history of *eros* and its present use in society today.

Eros is the perfect word for the love of Gnosticism, Existentialism, and Behaviorism. Each of these work together to define a life of self-awareness and self-centeredness driven by self-gratification. In *eros*, the desire for self-gratification is everything, even if it means the destruction of a relationship. Even when it rises to the higher plane of concern for others, it is still always measured by the yardstick of self: "What does this do for me?"

Genuine fulfillment in a relationship is difficult, if not impossible, when self is always at the center of that relationship. This is probably the main reason why the Holy Spirit led the New Testament writers to avoid the word completely. As this word best describes the love of the world, it is the least suited for use when referring to biblical love.

CHAPTER SEVEN

The Facets of Biblical Love

And one of them, a lawyer, asked Him [a question], testing Him, "Teacher, which is the great commandment in the Law?" And He said to him, "YOU SHALL LOVE THE LORD YOUR GOD WITH ALL YOUR HEART, AND WITH ALL YOUR SOUL, AND WITH ALL YOUR MIND." This is the great and foremost commandment. The second is like it, "YOU SHALL LOVE YOUR NEIGHBOR AS YOURSELF." On these two commandments depend the whole Law and the Prophets. (Matthew 22:35–40)

L ove is the central theme in both the Old and New Testaments. It is through love as God revealed it to us in His Word and through His Son, Jesus Christ, that we are able to overcome the damage caused by sin. Through biblical love, we are able to build healthy relationships. Love should form the foundation of every relationship, so that in spite of failures in those relationships, we are able to stay together and overcome those failures. In order to do that, we must learn to distinguish between the false love of the world and the true love taught in the Bible. This is why we must put aside the thought that sex is love. In marriage, sex is an act of loving obedience to God and to our spouse. This is true for both the husband and the wife. Genuine biblical love will lead to a healthy view of sex as the Creator intended it and will guard against the destructive forces of the false love of the world. Biblical love is the greatest force available to man to change himself and to change the world.

We do not have to understand everything the Bible teaches in order to express love biblically. All we need to know is that, if we will walk in the Spirit as God's Word commands us to do, we will love with God's love (Galatians 5:16). The purpose of this section is to explain how to distinguish false love from biblical love, how to apply biblical love to our relationships, and how to excel in biblical love.

One of Paul's most positive letters was written to the church at Thessalonica. He had a great relationship with them and enjoyed mutual respect and admiration together with them. He wrote:

> Now as to the love of the brethren, you have no need for [anyone] to write to you, for you yourselves are taught by God to love one another; for indeed you do practice it toward all the brethren who are in all Macedonia. But we urge you, brethren, to excel still more. (1 Thessalonians 4:9–10)

There are two facets to biblical love: obedience to God, and being genuine friends with God and with each other. We need to understand both aspects in order to excel.

FACET 1: AGAPE

The most prevalent Greek term translated "love" in the New Testament is *agape*. *Agape* is the noun form, and *agapao* is the verb. To avoid confusion, when I am speaking of the entire word group, I will refer to it as *agape*. Because the word is used so extensively in the New Testament, we must examine it from several different directions to gain a clear understanding of its meaning. Cremer wrote:

> Now, we find agape used to designate a love unknown to writers outside of the New Testament . . . *love in its fullest conceivable form*; love as it is the distinguishing attribute, not of humanity, but, in the strictest sense, of Divinity.[1]

Bishop Trench wrote:

> For it would not be forgotten that agape is a word born within the bosom of revealed religion: it occurs in the Septuagint (2 Sam. xiii. 15; Cant. ii. 4; Jer. ii.2), and the Apocrypha (Wisd. iii. 9); but there is no trace of it in any heathen writer whatever, and as little in Philo and Josephus.[2]

Some are now disputing the exclusivity of this word prior to the Septuagint and the New Testament. However, no one has been able to establish a wide use of the word until the New Testament. Its frequency in the New Testament—used over 350 times—is of greater significance than the lack of frequency before the New Testament because its frequency provides a well-rounded context from which to draw its meaning.

Both the noun and the verb are never joined with other words to form new words, as is the case with *philia*, the second word group we will look at in this section. Therefore, the meaning of *agape* is easier to understand when the Scriptures form the basis of our study, rather than the preconceived ideas transported from the world.

Agape Reflects the Nature of the One Expressing It

Most discussions of *agape* begin by stating that *agape* is a love that does not take into consideration the worthiness of the object to which it is given and that it is sacrificial love. These are what *agape* does in certain circumstances. However, neither statement alone nor together defines it.

In some passages in the New Testament, we see that *agape* is used for worldly love, that it is sometimes directed to objects because of their perceived worth to the one who loves them, and that in some circumstances there is no self-sacrifice involved. Therefore, the unworthiness of the object and the sacrifice in the act of love are not definitions but applications of *agape*.

Concerning its meaning, Leon Morris wrote, "Agape is spontaneous love, love freely given and not elicited by anything in the loved one."[3] Wuest appears to differ with that when he wrote:

> "Agapao" speaks of a love which is awakened by a sense of value in an object which causes one to prize it. It springs from an apprehension of the preciousness of an object. It is a love of esteem and approbation. *The quality of this love is determined by the character of the one who loves, and that of the object loved.*[4] (Italics mine)

What is important to see in this statement is that, of all of the Greek words associated with love, *agape* is first and foremost the love that most reflects the nature of the one who expresses it. This is the underlying thought in John 3:16, "For God so loved the world, that He gave His only begotten Son, that whoever believes in Him should not perish, but have eternal life." What is in view is not the character of the object of the love but the character of the One who loves.

In a number of passages, this definition of *agape* is very important to understanding the text. Jesus taught:

> But I say to you, love your enemies, and pray for those who persecute you, in order that *you may be* sons of your Father who is in heaven; for He causes His sun to rise on [the] evil and [the] good, and sends rain on [the] righteous and [the] unrighteous. (Matthew 5:44–45, italics mine)

The phrase "you may be" translates the term *ginomai* in the Greek text. W. E. Vine listed no less than twenty-one different ways the King James Version translates *ginomai*. Albert Barnes explained the meaning of the term in this context, ". . . in doing good to enemies, they resemble God."[5] Therefore, the meaning of the passage is that loving our enemies demonstrates a character like God's character, because He also loves His enemies.

In another passage, Jesus rebuked the unbelieving Jews when He said:

> If God were your Father, you would love Me, for I proceeded forth and have come from God. . . . You are of [your] father the devil, and you want to do the desires of your father. He was a murderer from the beginning, and does not stand in the truth because there is no truth in him. Whenever he speaks a lie, he speaks from his own [nature] for he is a liar, and the father of lies. (John 8:42, 44)

Those unbelieving Jews did not love Jesus, because, being born of a different father, they did not have the character of the Heavenly Father. This aspect of *agape*, that its expression reveals one's true character, is consistent throughout the New Testament and is basic to understanding the concept.

Agape Is an Act of the Will

Not only does *agape* reflect the nature of the one expressing it, but *agape* is an act of the will. Cremer wrote,

"Agapan is used in all places where the direction of the will is the point to be considered."[6] Wherever the English word *love* is commanded in the New Testament, it is *agape,* because *agape* is an act of the will—a choice made. No other Greek word associated with love fits this definition as clearly as *agape.*

The idea that *agape* is a choice can be seen in many passages. For instance, "And if you love those who love you, what credit is [that] to you? For even sinners love those who love them" (Luke 6:32). Notice how much fuller the meaning of that verse is when it is paraphrased: "If you *choose to* love those who *choose to* love you, what credit is that to you? For even sinners *choose to* love those who *choose to* love them." This brings out the sense of personal responsibility in choosing to love, and it helps us understand the full implications of the verse.

In Luke 11:43, the Pharisees "love [*agapao*] the . . . respectful greetings in the market places." However, note that Luke recorded another instance (20:46) when Jesus said, "Beware of the scribes, who . . . love [*phileo*] respectful greetings in the market places." We will be studying in depth the Greek word *phileo* in the next chapter. Here, we see that, by comparing these similar contexts and noting the change, we are able to arrive at a fuller understanding of both passages.

In the first instance, in Luke 11, Jesus emphasized that the Pharisees had decided as an act of their will to love respectful greetings. In the second instance, Luke 20, Jesus emphasized that the scribes find the respectful greetings attractive to them. The former is a condemnation delivered to the guilty party for a wrong choice. The latter is a warning given to the people to avoid being like the guilty party who find respectful greetings attractive to them.

Agape Is an Act of Obedience to God

For the Christian, it is a small step from *agape* as a choice to *agape* as an act of obedience. Yet further reflection will show that in practice it is a giant step. Obeying is one of the hardest things for us to do, because of the Fall in the Garden of Eden. It is the transformation from a character of disobedience to a character of obedience that is at the heart of our salvation in Christ. One whose heart has not been changed has not been born again. John wrote:

> And by this we know that we have come to know Him, if we keep His commandments. The one who says, "I have come to know Him," and does not keep His commandments, is a liar, and the truth is not in him; but whoever keeps His word, in him the love of God has truly been perfected. By this we know that we are in Him." (1 John 2:3–5)

If we are born again, then the one small step we need to take is to yield ourselves to the power of the Holy Spirit and through Him to simply obey what the Bible tells us to do. This is what the Bible means when it commands us to "walk in the Spirit" (Galatians 5:16).

Love as an act of obedience to God is clear in several New Testament passages. Jesus said, "If you love

Me, you will keep My commandments" (John 14:15).
In this statement, *agape* is seen as an act of obedience.
Love for Jesus means a willingness to obey Him. In
order to be sure His disciples understood that statement, He reversed it later in the same context, "He who
has My commandments and keeps them he it is who
loves Me. . . ." (John 14:21).

The time of this action is in the future. It applies to a
time after the cross and after the ascension, when Jesus'
followers will demonstrate their faith by their love. The
obedience referred to, and hence, the love enjoined, will
require knowledge of His will.

Agape Requires Being Born Again

At this point, it is essential that we carefully think
through the New Testament teaching regarding *agape*.
Whenever we talk about knowledge with reference to
salvation and the Christian experience, we must be careful not to get the cart before the horse or we will end up
with Gnosticism. Remember that we are not saved by
knowledge. We know because we are saved. In the same
way, we do not love, *agape*, on the basis of knowledge.

When Jesus said that His disciples would demonstrate
their love for Him by their obedience to His will, He was
not suggesting that love is the act of knowing His will.
That would suggest a Gnostic love. Also, if Jesus is no
longer present, how could they or any future disciple
obey Him? The answer is found in the same context.
The Comforter, the Spirit of Truth, will come to make
known the will of Jesus to them. In this way, Jesus said

the disciples "shall know that I am in My Father, and you in Me, and I in you" (John 14:20). The Holy Spirit is the One who makes obedience possible. Through the power of the Holy Spirit, it is possible to both have and keep His commandments and thereby love Him.

So we see that when the New Testament speaks of love as obedience, it assumes that the individual expressing the love has the Holy Spirit, who enables conformity to the Divine will. Jesus said:

> But the Helper, the Holy Spirit, whom the Father will send in My name, He will teach you all things, and bring to your remembrance all that I said to you. (John 14:26)

> When the Helper comes, whom I will send to you from the Father, [that is] the Spirit of truth who proceeds from the Father, He will bear witness of Me. (John 15:26)

> But when He, the Spirit of truth, comes, He will guide you into all the truth; for He will not speak on His own initiative, but whatever He hears, He will speak; and He will disclose to you what is to come. He shall glorify Me, for He shall take of Mine and shall disclose [it] to you. All things that the Father has are Mine; therefore I said that He takes of Mine and will disclose [it] to you. (John 16:13–15)

The person who is by nature obedient is born again and has learned how to walk in the Spirit. This is what

Paul meant when he taught that the fruit of the Spirit is love (Galatians 5:22). John expressed this in a different way when he wrote, "everyone who loves is born of God and knows God" (1 John 4:7). Clearly, in this passage the concept of *agape* has progressed from a matter of personal choice to conformity to the divine will, which is made possible by rebirth and the control of the Holy Spirit.

Agape May Be an Act of Self-Sacrifice

Many commentators start by defining *agape* as personal sacrifice and loving the unlovely. Masumi Toyotome calls *agape* the "in spite of" kind of love.

> The person is loved "in spite of," not because of, what he is. One may be the most ugly, most wretched, most debased person in the world and would still be loved when he meets this "in spite of" kind of love. . . . He may seem absolutely worthless, and yet he would be loved as though he were of infinite worth.[7]

Undoubtedly Toyotome had in mind verses such as Romans 5:8, where Paul wrote, "But God demonstrates His own love toward us, in that while we were yet sinners, Christ died for us."

Nygren followed the same line of thinking when he delineated the content of divine love in the following outline:

1. *Agape* is spontaneous and "unmotivated" (i.e., not out of self-need)

2. *Agape* is "indifferent to value" (i.e., not regarding the value of the object loved)
3. *Agape* is creative (i.e., that *agape* loves and imparts value by loving)
4. *Agape* is the initiator of fellowship (i.e., that God's love is the only way for man to enter into fellowship with God)[8]

Both Toyotome and Nygren are correct if they are speaking of what *agape* does as an act of obedience to the divine will. However, it is misleading to say that these are definitions of *agape*. To do so is to place *agape* far above the daily existence of the average Christian. Love does not always have to be spontaneous and unmotivated to be *agape*. *Agape* is not always "in spite of."

Agape may be expressed toward an object in spite of the unworthiness of the object to receive it. However, that is not always true of divine love. Jesus said, "For this reason the Father loves Me, because I lay down My life that I may take it again" (John 10:17). Here we see that even in divine love, it is at times "because of."

Concerning this, Robertson wrote:

> For this reason (dia touto). Points to the following hoti clause. The Father's love for the Son is drawn out (John 3:16) by the voluntary offering of the Son for the sin of the world (Romans 5:8). Hence the greater exaltation (Philippians 2:9).[9]

One cannot, therefore, press Nygren's outline in every context. His point is better seen as a secondary, rather than a primary, meaning of *agape*. The primary meaning is that *agape* is the expression of one's nature as an act of the will in obedience to God.

Many today labor under the misconception that in order to love with *agape*, one must give up something dear for someone else. That is not only a misconception of the biblical concept of sacrifice; it is a misconception of *agape*. A sacrifice in the Bible is not something that one gives up against his will or at great personal expense. A sacrifice is giving something willingly out of a heart of obedience and gratitude to God.

John wrote, "For this is the love of God, that we keep His commandments; and His commandments are not burdensome" (1 John 5:3). It is possible that God may choose for some to pay a great price or even die for their faith as an expression of their love for Him. At times, *agape* is demonstrated this way. However, when this happens it is not because the essence of *agape* is self-denial or personal loss. It is because the essence of *agape* is obedience to God.

Carl Henry wrote:

> Unrecompensed love is to structure the whole of life as the Divine command. The moral agent will promote at the same time his own best interest and that of his fellow man by doing the will of God. In love the supreme interests of all men coincide. . . . Ewing rather humorously evaluated it: "In sharp contrast to even the higher egoism and still more to egoistic hedonism the ethical view properly preached in Christian countries has usually been

that the primary virtue is unselfishness viewed as the readiness to sacrifice oneself for other men. But this view cannot, any more than egoistic hedonism, be carried to its absolute extreme. A society in which everybody spent his life sacrificing all his pleasure for others would be even more absurd than a society whose members all lived by taking in each other's washing." A major weakness of this stress on self-sacrifice is its lack of assurance that the individual's own interests are really preserved in the promotion of those others. . . . Love holds the interest of the self and of others together.[10]

Therefore, the primary meaning of *agape* is that it is a love of the will that reflects the nature of the one who expresses it. It involves a choice. For the believer, the choice is based upon knowledge of and obedience to the divine will of God. Additional considerations, such as the unworthiness of the object or the self-sacrifice of the giver, are secondary to the primary meaning.

Notice how this clarification of the definition of *agape* helps to better understand one significant passage of Scripture, 1 John 3:16–17.

We know love by this, that He laid down His life [*psuche*] for us; and we ought to lay down our lives [*psuche*] for the brethren. But whoever has the world's goods, and beholds his brother in need and closes his heart against him, how does the love of God abide in him? (1 John 3:16–17)

The love of Jesus led Him to give up His physical life by dying on the cross for us. This was an act of obedience to the will of God the Father. However, the Greek term in the passage is *psuche*, which could be translated "soul." In the chapter on Behaviorism, we noted that in some contexts *psuche* means more than mere immaterial existence. It refers to the essence of the person, his motives, attitude, and desires. It is the force behind his personal expectations and goals. Basically setting aside *psuche* means setting aside our personal interests for the benefit of others. It may or may not require personal sacrifice, but it does require putting the interests of others above our own interests. In 1 John 3, the meaning is to be willing to share with a brother in need what God has given to us. It only means personal sacrifice if it is God's will.

Once we see these basic elements of *agape*, it is not difficult to understand the concept. Since it is the most basic of human responses to God's love and is a result of God working in our lives, this definition will suffice. *Agape* reflects the nature of the one giving it, it is an act of the will, it is an act of obedience to the will of God, and it is made possible by being born again. Later, we will learn more about *agape* as we compare it to *philia* and its cognates in the New Testament.

FACET 2: PHILIA

A second Greek word that forms the basis for biblical love is *philia*. *Philia*, the noun, is used only a few times in the Greek New Testament and is translated "friendship." Another noun, *philos*, is translated "friend." The verb form, *phileo*, is the most frequent form found in the New Testament. *Philia* is combined with other words to form numerous new words. Because of the limit of time and space, we are not able to study each of those new words even though they form a significant part of God's revelation to us. Finally, *philia* is never commanded, because it is a response to the object loved and is drawn out by a relationship to that object. It will become obvious why that is so as we observe the development of the concept in Scripture.

Because *philia* and its cognates are used so extensively in the New Testament, and because they form such an important part of the Christian experience, we need to study a number of contexts in order to derive the meaning of this word group.

John's Gospel is the best place to start when seeking an understanding of *philia* in the New Testament. John used words like golden threads woven together to form a beautiful tapestry of the life and ministry of Jesus. By tracing the nouns *philia* and *philos* and the verb *phileo* in the Gospel of John, we discover their basic meaning and why they are so important to human relationships. To avoid confusion, when I am referring to the word group, I will refer to it as *philia*.

Philia Refers to Biblical Friendship

John introduced *philia* in chapter 3 in a dialogue between John the Baptist and his disciples regarding the ministry of Jesus. John's disciples displayed a hint of jealousy when they noted that the disciples of Jesus were baptizing more individuals than they were. John the Baptist was in prison, and his disciples came to him to complain about what Jesus and His disciples were doing. John the Baptist replied,

> "He who has the bride is the bridegroom; but the friend [*philos*] of the bridegroom, who stands and hears him, rejoices greatly because of the bridegroom's voice. And so this joy of mine has been made full." (John 3:29)

In this way, John was expressing his reaction to the ministry of Jesus. Because he was a friend of the bridegroom, that is a friend of Jesus, John rejoiced to see the response of the people to His ministry. This is true biblical friendship and, as we shall see, is what we earlier referred to as a relationship of fulfillment. Friendship in the biblical sense is far deeper and far more meaningful than friendship in our culture today. How one comes to this place in a relationship requires further study of the use of *philia* in John's Gospel.

Philia Involves Self-Disclosure

The second time *philia* is found is in chapter 5. The apostle John noted that Jesus taught, "For the Father loves [*phileo*] the Son, and shows Him all things that He Himself is doing; and greater works than these will He show Him, that you may marvel" (John 5:20). Note in this context that the concept of self-disclosure is introduced into the meaning of *philia*. This aspect of *philia*—self-disclosure—is repeated several times in the book. Self-disclosure in a relationship can be good or bad, beneficial or harmful, depending upon the situation. In both relationships of circumstance and relationships of purpose, it may not be wise to disclose too much of ourselves. However, we cannot achieve relationships of fulfillment without self-disclosure. Applying the principle of self-disclosure further, to disclose to someone else what was disclosed in a relationship of fulfillment may be a violation of that relationship and may damage or destroy that relationship. We will discuss this further in chapter 9.

Philia Involves Affection

The next time we find *philia* used in John's Gospel is in chapter 11. Lazarus is sick and about to die, and the sisters of Lazarus send a messenger to Jesus to ask Him to intervene. In verse 3 John tells us that they appealed to Jesus on the basis of His friendship with Lazarus. Their message was, "Lord, behold, he whom You love [*phileo*] is sick" (John 11:3). It is correct to ascribe here all of the positive emotions that warm friendship suggests, including attraction, affinity, and affection.

A significant distinction between *agape* and *philia* can be seen in the apostle's editorial comment in verse 5, where John wrote, "Now Jesus loved [*agapao*] Martha, and her sister, and Lazarus" (John 11:5). This observation by John explained that, while Jesus loved (*phileo*)

Lazarus, which was the basis of the sisters' appeal to Him for help, Jesus also loved (*agapao*) Lazarus with a love that was consistent with the Heavenly Father's will. Jesus made this clear in His reply to the sisters when He said, "This sickness is not unto death, but for the glory of God, that the Son of God may be glorified by it" (John 11:4). Therefore, even though His actions in allowing Lazarus to die did not appear to be motivated by love (*philia*), they were consistent with love (*agape*).

Philia Must Yield to Agape

The play on the Greek terms for love in John 11 presents a very important principle with reference to biblical love. Choosing to do God's will for others (*agape*) must supersede what affectionate friendship (*philia*) might otherwise lead us to do. This does not mean that *agape* is a better, or purer, or higher form of love, or that *philia* is somehow inferior or defective. As we will see in the next chapter, the two concepts should be viewed as two facets of the one concept: biblical love.

John underscores the richness of the two aspects of *phileo*, self-disclosure and affection, in one of the most intimate settings in the New Testament, the Last Supper in the upper room.

In John 15, Jesus explained to His disciples:

> If you abide in Me, and My words abide in you, ask whatever you wish, and it shall be done for you. By this is My Father glorified, that you bear much fruit, and [so] prove to be My disciples. Just as the

Father has loved [*agapao*] Me, I have also loved [*agapao*] you; abide in My love [*agapao*]. If you keep My commandments, you will abide in My love [*agapao*]; just as I have kept My Father's commandments and abide in His love [*agapao*]. These things I have spoken to you that My joy may be in you, and [that] your joy may be made full. This is My commandment, that you love [*agapao*] one another, just as I have loved [*agapao*] you. Greater love [*agapao*] has no one than this, that one lay down his life for his friends [*philos*]. You are My friends [*philos*] if you do what I command you. No longer do I call you slaves, for the slave does not know what his master is doing; but I have called you friends [*philos*], for all things that I have heard from My Father I have made known to you. You did not choose Me, but I chose you, and appointed you, that you should go and bear fruit, and [that] your fruit should remain, that whatever you ask of the Father in My name He may give to you. This I command you, that you love [*agapao*] one another. If the world hates you, you know that it has hated Me before [it hated] you. If you were of the world, the world would love [*phileo*] its own; but because you are not of the world, but I chose you out of the world, therefore the world hates you. (John 15:7–19)

Again we have the play on words between *agape* and *philia* as we saw in John 11. Here we learn more about the distinction between these two concepts, and hence, begin to understand the richness of biblical love and the important role it plays in our relationships with each other.

In the context of John 15 we find the metaphor of the grapevine. It describes our relationship to Jesus as a branch—as a part of a vine. The purpose of the relationship is to bear fruit. Only when we abide in the vine, Jesus Christ, are we able to bear fruit. As the chapter unfolds, we begin at the level of a relationship of purpose. Then we see that there is a fuller and deeper purpose: answered prayer. This leads to a relationship of fulfillment on the part of both Jesus and His disciples because the vine—that is, the vine and the branches together—bears fruit. To explain the connection between fruit bearing and prayer, Jesus used a play on the two word groups *agape* and *philia*.

To begin with, abiding in the vine means obeying the words of Jesus. This obedience is the result of a genuine love for the Savior, even as He sets the example for us by obeying and loving His Heavenly Father. It is this obedient love for the Father that led Jesus to lay down His life (*psuche*) for us, His friends. At this point, the subject shifts from obedient love to affectionate love. Jesus describes His relationship with those who obey Him, and hence, who love Him. The relationship deepens into friendship, which, in turn, is marked by self-disclosure. This is the same principle we saw in chapter 5 in the relationship between the Father and the Son with the Father disclosing all things to the Son.

The quality of friendship here is so far above what the world considers friendship that there is little comparison. It is not only a willingness to communicate completely with the one who is the object of our affection, it also means that we would even lay down our lives (*psuche*) for that person. It is at this point that self-sacrifice becomes meaningful. To willfully lay down one's life (*psuche*) for another person with whom there is no meaningful relationship is not only foolish, it is repugnant. But to lay down one's life (*psuche*) for someone with whom there is an affectionate relationship is an example of the highest level of relationship a human can experience.

This does not mean that heroism is wrong. There are many stories of individuals laying down their lives for another person in a moment before there is time to think. The goodness of the person produces quick action that could lead to personal injury or even death. However, this is usually a spur-of-the-moment impulse. There was little forethought, and so it cannot be classified as a well-thought-out decision. In fact, if the person had stopped to consider the results of the action, he may not have done what he did that led to his own injury or death.

Paul described this kind of earthly heroism when he wrote, "For one will hardly die for a righteous man; though perhaps for the good man someone would dare even to die" (Romans 5:7). Jesus' death on the cross was not heroism; it was a reasoned decision. Neither was it merely a sacrificing of self for someone who does not deserve it. It was an act of obedience to the Father, who chose to love the world by allowing His Son to die on the cross so that the world could be saved.

In John 15, we find another purpose for the decision Jesus made to give His life (psuche) for the world. The cross was for the purpose of establishing a relationship of affection with those who would be saved by this act of obedience to the Father. This is why Jesus calls those who obey Him "friends." Genuine biblical friendship is a relationship of fulfillment.

Now that we have defined biblical love from the standpoint of *agape* and *philia*, we need to put these two concepts together and see how they help us build relationships of fulfillment.

CHAPTER EIGHT

Biblical Love Expressed in Relationships

In the preceding chapter, we saw that biblical love has two facets: *agape* and *philia*. *Agape* reflects the nature of the one giving it, is an act of the will, is expressed as obedience to God, and, to be biblical, requires that the one giving it be born again. *Philia* is the act of self-disclosure to the one who is the object of genuine affection, which produces fulfillment in the relationship. In chapter 7, the purpose was to break down the concept of biblical love into its individual parts. In this chapter, our purpose is to put those parts back together to show how they form one concept—biblical love. We will then see how, when applied to our relationships, this concept will help us overcome the false philosophies of the world and the damage caused to our relationships by the false love of the world based upon those philosophies.

BIBLICAL LOVE REQUIRES BOTH AGAPE AND PHILIA

I have referred to *agape* and *philia* as two facets of love. As one diamond has many facets, biblical love has two: *agape* and *philia*. The important thing is to realize that *agape* and *philia*, two separate word groups in the Greek language, are not two totally unrelated kinds of love. Either one without the other forms a warped and even harmful form of love that is not biblical.

Perhaps the simplest way to explain this is to start with *philia*. When we allow ourselves to express *philia*—self-disclosure leading to deep affection without the anchor of obedience to God, which is the expression of *agape*—we fall into all kinds of harmful situations. When young people begin to date and share things about themselves they should not, the result is not the beautiful expression of affection made possible by biblical love. It becomes overpowering passion, which leads to the most harmful kinds of behavior. If the relationship is not destroyed, it is ruined. Even if the couple goes on to marry, the relationship will be scarred for life and is redeemable only by the mercy of God.

The same is true of married people in an office situation. If the individuals who are not married to each other begin to share intimate matters about their lives that ought not to be shared, the havoc this will reap on many lives is astronomical.

One more example will help to shed light on the need to keep *philia* with *agape* in relationships. I have served as a pastor for several congregations and visited many more. Some congregations are warm and friendly but closed to outsiders. The reason for this is, probably without knowing it, they major on *philia* in their fellowship. Everybody knows everybody else. Their love for each other is apparent in the good works they do for each other. However, when a visitor comes into their meeting, he or she never feels welcome, particularly if he or she is of another race, ethnicity, or has a personal problem the congregation is not prepared to handle.

Philia, as one facet of biblical love, must rest upon the firm foundation of obedience to God found in *agape*. *Agape* motivates change from the comfortable. *Agape* reaches out to form new relationships where none existed before. *Agape* requires going the second mile to overcome the tensions of building new relationships. *Agape* visits the fatherless and the widows in order to meet their needs, even when it won't add new members to the church. *Agape* patiently endures the unbeliever or new believer who does not understand how to behave in the household of God. An effective local church will have a balance between *agape* and *philia* in their fellowship. Without *agape, philia* becomes tepid *storge*, a weakened, ineffective response to others in unfulfilling relationships.

Agape must form the foundation of every relationship. Yet *agape* without *philia* also produces difficulty in relationships and can even destroy them.

Agape without *philia* quickly loses its bearings and ceases to be obedience to God. The zeal to accomplish the goals of the kingdom quickly becomes personal ambition to build castles in the sand. *Philia*, while focused on the objects of our affection, must always have God and affection for Him as the ultimate motivation. Without *philia*, we cease to have affection for God or for the immediate objects of our love. Service becomes drudgery. Relationships, even our relationship with God, become empty husks far short of the potential for fulfillment God intended.

This was the purpose of the dialogue between Peter and Jesus on the seashore after His resurrection (John 21:15–18). Peter, only a few days before and only hours before His trial and crucifixion, bragged about his love for Jesus by loudly proclaiming he would follow Him to death. Then, in the moment of truth, he denied Him repeatedly. Even after the resurrection, Peter left his vigil and, taking the other disciples with him, went back to his fishing boats.

What Peter needed was an infusion of biblical love, not just blind obedience. He needed a deep affection for the Savior based upon a heart of obedience that would endure the trials ahead of him in life. He needed an affection that would carry him through to the end. It is interesting to note that Jesus dropped the name Peter, which He gave to him the first time He met him. Jesus added the reference to Peter's physical birth by calling him son of John, rather than son of God. This was a subtle way of reminding Peter that, apart from Christ, he was no rock. He was only a lump of clay.

Jesus began by asking, "Simon, son of John, do you love [*agapao*] me?"

Peter, knowing the difference between the two facets of love, replied, "Yes, Lord; You know that I love [*phileo*] You." *Agape*, to Peter, was merely a foundation, a starting place. His denial proved that his desire to obey was not enough. He was determined to add the second facet, affection, to his love, which would form a love hard and enduring as a diamond.

Jesus asked a second time, "Simon, son of John, do you love [*agapao*] me?

Peter answered, "Yes, Lord, You know the I love [*phileo*] You." The first answer to the first question simply stated the fact of Peter's love. It was more than *agape*. It was *philia*. The second question, the same in content, now drew out of Peter an affirmation that he understood the question and, in His mind, he had given the correct answer.

Jesus asked a third question. In English, it appears that He asks the same question the third time and that is why Peter was grieved. However, it was a different question, and it was the first time Jesus asked it. "Simon, son of John, do you love [*phileo*] me?" Peter's expressed grief was because now Jesus was questioning not only his desire to obey, He was questioning his affection for Jesus, which would be necessary for Peter in order for him to endure the trials of ministry ahead of him. With broken spirit and contrite heart, Peter cried out to Jesus, "Lord, You know all things; You know that I love [*phileo*] You." Jesus' next statement confirmed that He did know that Peter would one day put *agape* and *philia* together and that he would be an effective messenger of the gospel:

Truly, truly, I say to you, when you were younger, you used to gird yourself, and walk wherever you wished; but when you grow old, you will stretch out your hands, and someone else will gird you, and bring you where you do not wish to [go.] (John 21:18)

History records that in the last moments of Peter's life, *agape* and *philia* enabled him to be martyred in a manner that brought honor and glory to his Lord and Savior.

Paul, on several occasions, spent time with Peter. Perhaps Peter shared this dialogue with Paul and this is what Paul had in mind when he wrote the conclusion to his letter to the church at Corinth, the Book of First Corinthians. He wrote, "If anyone does not love [*philia*] the Lord, let him be accursed. Maranatha" (1 Corinthians 16:22). With all of the instruction regarding love in this epistle, this is the only occurrence of *philia*. The conclusion I draw from it is that *agape*, the love of obedience, was necessary to change their behavior and resolve the problems in the church at Corinth. *Philia*, affection for Jesus Christ, was necessary to motivate them to follow through to full, complete reconciliation among themselves, with Paul, and with God.

The world often depicts love as a flame. This is an accurate metaphor when we realize that *agape* is the oil for the flame and *philia* produces the heat. Too much oil and the flame will go out. Not enough oil and the flame will go out. Too much heat and the flame will go out. Not enough heat and the flame will also go out. Biblical love is a balance between *agape* and *philia*. God makes this possible through new birth, the power of the Holy

Spirit, and His Word. We must apply these principles to our relationships.

Biblical Love Experienced

Remember in John 3 when the disciples of John the Baptist complained to John that the disciples of Jesus were baptizing more disciples than they were? John the Baptist's response was to rejoice in the pleasure the Bridegroom was receiving from His bride. We again find this thought of rejoicing in connection with biblical love in John 14–17:

> You heard that I said to you, "I go away, and I will come to you." If you loved Me, you would have rejoiced, because I go to the Father; for the Father is greater than I. (John 14:28)

> These things I have spoken to you, that My joy may be in you, and [that] your joy may be made full. (John 15:11)

> Truly, truly, I say to you, that you will weep and lament, but the world will rejoice; you will be sorrowful, but your sorrow will be turned to joy. Whenever a woman is in travail she has sorrow, because her hour has come; but when she gives birth to the child, she remembers the anguish no more, for joy that a child has been born into the world. Therefore you too now have sorrow; but I will see you again, and your heart will rejoice, and no one takes your joy away from you. And in that day you will ask Me

no question. Truly, truly, I say to you, if you shall ask the Father for anything, He will give it to you in My name. Until now you have asked for nothing in My name; ask and you will receive, that your joy may be made full. (John 16:20–24)

But now I come to Thee; and these things I speak in the world, that they may have My joy made full in themselves. I have given them Thy word; and the world has hated them, because they are not of the world, even as I am not of the world. (John 17:13–14)

Chapters 13–17 of John's Gospel refer to the most intimate moments in human history, moments before Jesus died on the cross. In those moments, Jesus taught His disciples what they could expect in their relationship once He ascended to the Father and the Holy Spirit indwelled His church here on earth. It would be a relationship filled with joy because it would be a relationship characterized by biblical love now achieved through the cross and through the indwelling Holy Spirit.

I recently sat through a series of seminary classes taught over a period of two days and taught from the point of view of Existentialism. Each day began with the professor building a sense of existential angst— dread at how bad things were in the world—followed by a heavy emphasis on personal blame for the malaise and on individual responsibility to unite with some humanitarian cause to correct the problems. At no time was the Bible expounded or the doctrines of love and grace or the sovereign reign of Christ over human events presented. Both days ended with the professor and students alike drained. There were no expressions of joy over what God was doing in the world. What a contrast to the account of Jesus with His disciples in the upper room and on the way to the garden of Gethsemane! Even though the disciples were not yet joyful, because the baptism of the Holy Spirit had not yet taken place, Jesus experienced joy. His joy would become fuller as His followers experienced joy throughout the Church Age.

Christ died on the cross, rose from the dead, ascended back to heaven, and sent the Holy Spirit to empower the church and to implement changes by building relationships of fulfillment. The false philosophies of Gnosticism, Existentialism, and Behaviorism rob the church of its power to implement these changes, by destroying relationships or simply rendering them ineffective. Perhaps the greatest damage is that these philosophies rob Christians of the joy Jesus spoke about, this joy being the greatest expression of His glory here on earth.

BIBLICAL LOVE PUTS RESONSIBILITY BACK INTO RELATIONSHIPS

Armed with an overall view of the tapestry of John's Gospel woven with the threads of agape and philia, we are now equipped to better understand the intimate relationship in the upper room and on the way to Gethsemane, a relationship that prepared the disciples for a life of service to Him. It also helps us to understand how we can achieve relationships of fulfillment, which we are saved to enjoy.

The first characteristic of a relationship of fulfillment is that it is based upon biblical love. Biblical love involves the ability and willingness to fulfill our responsibilities in the relationship. Through biblical love, we are able to meet the needs of the other person in the relationship and, in return, to have our needs met through them. This aspect of a relationship of fulfillment sets it apart from relationships of circumstance, where the individuals with whom we have a relationship may never know we exist or that we are meeting their needs. In relationships of purpose, biblical love enables us to move beyond merely achieving goals to achieving genuine fulfillment in our relationships.

Biblical Love in Relationships of Circumstance

In relationships of circumstance, we love out of a heart of obedience, regardless of any return for our love. We love because it is the right thing to do. This truth has almost been lost in society because of the false philosophies of Gnosticism, Existentialism, and Behaviorism. For instance, I may have a marking pen as I walk down the street. Through some twisted logic that can be traced back to the false philosophies of Gnosticism, Existentialism, and Behaviorism, I might be expected to use my marking pen to deface public or private property. Graffiti has become a badge of the so-called "free thinkers."

Gnosticism says that there is no absolute truth, so I have a right to decide what I am going to do with my marking pen. Existentialism says that the world is ugly already, so a little more ugliness is all right. Besides, I have the right to define my existence any way I please. Behaviorism says I am really not responsible for my behavior. Defacing someone else's property is merely the expression of my natural instincts.

Those who deface the property of others sense no responsibility to protect that property. Nor do they accept responsibility for the damage done, not only to the property itself and its owners, but to society in general. Graffiti has to be one of the clearest examples of selfishness today.

However, in this example of a relationship of circumstance, the relationship between the property owners and me, biblical love would lead me to keep the marking pen in my pocket and walk on. In fact, it may even lead me to pick up some garbage blown on to the property by the wind. Whereas the graffiti writer performs his cowardly act in secret, biblical love would lead me to pick up the garbage even if the owner was not there to see it. This is *agape* at work. There is someone who sees it—God. If it is biblical love, it is done to please Him. It is not done to somehow earn merit. A child of God already has the full benefit of salvation. He merely needs to put it into practice in every relationship. Pleasing our Lord should be motivation enough to act responsibly, even in relationships of circumstance, where we do not expect to get anything in return.

Biblical Love in Relationships of Purpose

Remember that relationships of purpose are those relationships into which we enter by choice. We, and others in the relationship, have a purpose we want to accomplish when we enter it. Unlike relationships of circumstance, we do expect something in return for our efforts and the efforts of others in the relationship. The burden of acting responsibly in relationships of purpose is not greater than the burden of relationships of circumstances.

We must never come to the place in our relationships where we are only seeking to please men rather than God. Doing so opens us up to all types of temptations. Doing so also opens us up to tyranny, that is, allowing others to control our behavior instead of being motivated out of a desire to obey and please God. Seeking to please others amounts to slavery. Paul wrote, "It was for freedom that Christ set us free; therefore keep standing firm and do not be subject again to a yoke of slavery" (Galatians 5:1).

An amazing truth about biblical love is that it prevents us from ever being enslaved again. While it is true that people might put us under a form of bondage, it is equally true that those who have been set free from the bondage of sin can never again be enslaved by anyone. In Colossians 3:22–25, Paul explains this truth in these words:

> Slaves, in all things obey those who are your
> masters on earth, not with external service, as those

who [merely] please men, but with sincerity of heart, fearing the Lord. Whatever you do, do your work heartily, as for the Lord rather than for men, knowing that from the Lord you will receive the reward of the inheritance. It is the Lord Christ whom you serve. For he who does wrong will receive the consequences of the wrong which he has done, and that without partiality.

Slavery of men by men is, for the slave, a relationship of circumstance rather than a relationship of purpose. The New Testament has much to say about how Christians are to act when they find themselves in such a situation. Unlike the situational ethics of the false philosophies of Gnosticism, Existentialism, and Behaviorism, the responsibility to love biblically is still in force even when we are slaves of men.

Biblical Love Produces Fulfillment in Relationships

In relationships of circumstance, biblical love motivates us to do what is pleasing to God regardless of whether or not we receive any return from that relationship. We did not choose it, but we still love God and seek to obey Him by meeting our responsibilities in the relationship.

In relationships of purpose, biblical love motivates us to fulfill our responsibilities. We justifiably expect others in the relationship to meet our needs according to our contractual agreement. However, the ultimate motivation still is to please God. Then, even when others fail us, we still know that our Lord will meet our needs and reward us for our obedience. When we come to relationships of fulfillment, we see the greatest benefit from understanding how to express biblical love, a balance between *agape* and *philia*. In the next chapter we will see how biblical love, when properly expressed, brings fulfillment in our relationships.

CHAPTER NINE

The Crowning Achievement
of Biblical Love

BIBLICAL LOVE PRODUCES FULFILLMENT IN RELATIONSHIPS

Relationships of Fulfillment Require an Attitude of Servanthood

The upper room discourse in John chapter 13 begins with Jesus demonstrating *agape* to His disciples by performing the function of a servant by washing their feet. It was merely preliminary to the service He would render a few hours later by dying on the cross for them. In chapter 13, *agape* is commanded and is permanently bound to servanthood (John 13:34–35). No one can claim to be expressing biblical love, nor will they ever achieve the level of fulfillment in a relationship unless they first see themselves as servants in that relationship. Relationships of fulfillment begin with an attitude of servanthood on the part of both partners in the relationship.

Relationships of Fulfillment Require an Obedient Heart

We have already seen that John chapter 14 introduces the idea of obedience to God into the meaning of *agape*. Along with obedience is the promise of the Holy Spirit. We are not supposed to search within ourselves to find the will to obey. A heart of obedience is a gift from God and instilled in us by His Holy Spirit.

Any relationship, whether it begins as a relationship of circumstance or as a relationship of purpose, has the potential of becoming a relationship of fulfillment if both parties possess a heart of obedience that originates from and is empowered by the indwelling Holy Spirit.

Relationships of Fulfillment Accomplish Great Things for God

Jesus made a startling disclosure when He said:

> Believe Me that I am in the Father and the Father in Me; otherwise believe on account of the works themselves. Truly, truly, I say to you, he who believes in Me, the works that I do, shall he do also; and greater [works] than these shall he do; because I go to the Father. (John 14:11–12)

What an awesome promise! It is difficult to conceive of any work that would be greater than what Jesus did during His time on earth. Perhaps He will tell us what He meant during the great wedding feast of the Lamb. We will all be seated around His table dressed in white garments, the garments He has given us identified only as "the righteous acts of the saints," (Revelation 19:8). Without a doubt, our ability to reach the level of fulfillment in our relationships will have something to do with those works because it is in relationships of fulfillment that we most glorify Him.

Relationships of Fulfillment Enjoy an Enduring Peace

Before we leave John chapter 14, we need to notice one more truth that identifies a relationship of fulfillment. After Jesus taught about the coming Holy Spirit, Who would enable His disciples to obey Him, and after He promised that they would do greater works than He did, He said, "Peace I leave with you; My peace I give to you; not as the world gives, do I give to you. Let not your heart be troubled, nor let it be fearful" (John 14:27).

Following the topic of peace throughout the Old and New Testaments provides a rewarding study. Mankind is longing for peace, but there will never be peace without a personal relationship with Jesus Christ. Paul, when counseling two women involved in a conflict at Philippi, instructed them:

> Be anxious for nothing, but in everything by prayer and supplication with thanksgiving let your requests be made known to God. And the peace of God, which surpasses all comprehension, shall guard your hearts and your minds in Christ Jesus. Finally, brethren, whatever is true, whatever is honorable, whatever is right, whatever is pure, whatever is lovely, whatever is of good repute, if there is any ex-

cellence and if anything worthy of praise, let your mind dwell on these things. The things you have learned and received and heard and seen in me, practice these things; and the God of peace shall be with you. (Philippians 4:6–9)

James instructed Christians to consider God's wisdom:

But the wisdom from above is first pure, then peaceable, gentle, reasonable, full of mercy and good fruits, unwavering, without hypocrisy. And the seed whose fruit is righteousness is sown in peace by those who make peace. (James 3:17–18)

Relationships of fulfillment are opportunities for God's children to enjoy His peace as they relate to each other in the Body of Christ. It is a sad commentary today that many in the world appear to be enjoying a greater degree of peace than those in the family of God.

Relationships of Fulfillment Bear Fruit to the Glory of God

In John chapter 15 we have the metaphor of the vine and the branches of fruit. Many stumble over the passage because they want to read into it the concept of initial salvation. Perhaps what leads many astray is their view of branches. Study a grapevine. Where does the vine end and the branches begin? There is no distinct separation. The branches on a vine are part of the vine, not appendages. The same is true of the clusters of fruit. This is why Jesus used the metaphor. He was resting His expectation of glorifying the Father upon His relationship with His followers. We cannot bear fruit without Him, and, in a real sense, He cannot bear fruit without us.

The vine metaphor is a perfect illustration of relationships of fulfillment. Fulfillment involves mutual effort in the relationship so that both parties enjoy the fruit of that relationship to the glory of God.

Relationships of Fulfillment Involve Genuine Intimacy

We do not have many relationships in which we would want to, or that it would be wise to, divulge our inner thoughts. This is especially true in relationships of circumstance. Why would we want to entrust such a precious possession to someone who might tread it under foot like a pearl before a swine. Yet we live in a society where individuals are encouraged to do this everyday.

Full self-disclosure is usually not wise in relationships of purpose as well. While we should never misrepresent the truth about ourselves, neither are we required to tell all in every situation. It is like wearing clothes. Parts of our bodies need to be seen and parts of our bodies do not. The circumstances determine the amount we reveal. In a doctor's office, we might need to show more than in the swimming pool.

I realize that an illustration of clothing may seem a little overdone, but consider what is happening today. The natural inhibitions of people are being dismantled under the guise of personal freedom. As individuals walk about with more and more of their bodies exposed, they are also calling in to talk radio and television and going on stage to reveal more and more about themselves for the purpose of titillating a drooling public. Even Christian radio and television is promoting the public exposure of intimate details of relationships that serve only one purpose—satisfying the curiosity of those who have no right to see and hear what is presented.

If we are ever to achieve fulfillment in our relationships, we must learn what to share, when to share it, and with whom to share it. Only those who know how to share themselves properly with their partner will experience true fulfillment in that relationship.

A few months ago, while sitting in a doctor's office, I saw a portion of a daytime television program. I had never seen the program before—and hope I never see it again. The program had to do with forgiveness. The format consisted of an individual who had a secret to share that they had never shared with their partner. The individual was supposed to share the secret to a live television audience with the partner in another room and a caption of his or her face shown simultaneously as the secret was revealed. On that particular program, a wife revealed something she had never told her husband even though they had been married for several years. The secret was that she was still married to another man. The wife then moved to a large elaborate doorway and waited to see if her husband would step out and offer her his forgiveness.

I cannot image anything more destructive to a relationship, nor anything more horrifying than such a blatant disregard for the feelings and rights of the partner in a relationship. This couple probably received a lot of money to entertain the audience with this act of exhibitionism, but how could the relationship ever be restored once it has been so degraded? If we are ever to achieve fulfillment in our relationships, we must learn how to share intimacy so that it builds the relationship and does not violate it.

Relationships That Can Experience Fulfillment

What kinds of relationships are there in which we can expect to reach relationships of fulfillment? The most obvious relationship is our relationship with the three persons of the Godhead. Next would be a marriage relationship. But these do not exhaust the possibilities. We should be able to reach a level of fulfillment with almost anyone who is born again and with whom we share biblical love.

A Relationship of Fulfillment with God

We must start this list with God. It is God who makes possible any relationship of fulfillment. It was popular a few years ago to speak of the "I/Thou" relationship, which meant that we needed to identify who we are in order to identify who God is. This was the call of the existentialist who claimed to be a Christian to a world blinded by angst or dread.

The Bible, when properly understood, presents the opposite view. When we see God as He has revealed Himself to us in His Word, we will be able to discover who we are. When we begin with a relationship of fulfillment with God, we will then be able to establish relationships of fulfillment with each other.

A Relationship of Fulfillment in Marriage

Moses said that Adam and Eve would become one flesh in the Garden of Eden. We are never told in the Old Testament what the one-flesh relationship was like. The next time we find the concept is in the Gospels, where Jesus taught on the subject of divorce. While there is still much disagreement on the exact implication of His teaching, one thing is sure, adultery and fornication destroy a one-flesh relationship.

Ephesians 5:22–33 is the only place where we find an explanation of what a one-flesh relationship is. We can see that the one-flesh relationship is like the relationship between Christ and His church. The reason why it was not explained before was because the relationship between Christ and His church had never been revealed before. Just as the relationship between Christ and His church requires obedience and serving, so the one-flesh relationship requires obedience and serving. In a God-honoring marriage, the one-flesh relationship is the ultimate expression of a relationship of fulfillment between human beings in this life.

Now that we have the full revelation of the relationship between Christ and His church, one would think every Christian marriage would achieve this level of fulfillment. Yet statistics show otherwise. Why is it that divorce among Christians is almost as frequent as among non-Christians? It is because Christians are building their marriages on the failed philosophies of the world and the false love of fallen man instead of upon the Word of God and biblical love. Because of this families are torn apart, society lacks a clear witness regarding the truth of Christ, and the Savior is not receiving the glory He deserves. We need to tune out the false philosophies of the world and return to the Bible for the pattern for our one-flesh relationships. Then our marriages will reach the level of fulfillment made possible by Christ.

Relationships of Fulfillment between
Individuals of the Same Sex

Not only do the false philosophies of the world prevent individuals from enjoying a relationship of fulfillment with God and fulfillment in marriage, they prevent individuals from enjoying relationships of fulfillment with members of the same sex. Homosexuality has been around since the beginning of time, and the Bible clearly condemns it. However, now that absolute truth has been dispensed with, now that society dictates what are acceptable relationships rather than the Word of God, and now that behaviorists have determined to their satisfaction that homosexuality is merely an acceptable alternative lifestyle because individuals are born that way, having a relationship of fulfillment with a member of the same sex is very difficult.

On the one hand, individuals of the same sex are afraid to draw close into relationships of fulfillment because of the stigma placed on it by society. If two men appear to be enjoying a close relationship with each other, they are automatically labeled gay. On the other hand, by teaching that homosexuality is an acceptable lifestyle, and that it is one a person cannot avoid because he is born that way, those who are entrapped in it have little hope of overcoming it, even if they want to. They have been preconditioned by society to think, act, and feel like a homosexual. The false philosophies of Gnosticism, Existentialism, and Behaviorism work together to reinforce an addictive behavior learned either by accident or taught to them by someone preying upon them.

The good news is that such falsehood can be refuted with the truth. Sinful sexual behavior is not unique to our society. Individuals can escape enslavement to addictive sexual behavior, whether it be homosexuality, pedophilia, pornography, or any other pattern of behavior inconsistent with God's revealed will. Those who are born again and in whom the Holy Spirit dwells are declared to be temples for holy service to God.

Many societies throughout history were destroyed by the gangrene of godless uncontrolled sexual behavior. None was more decadent than Roman culture, especially at Corinth, where the temple to Aphrodite, the love goddess, was the cultural centerpiece. It is said that there were one thousand prostitutes in the city when Paul visited. To the Christians, Paul wrote:

Do you not know that your bodies are members of Christ? Shall I then take away the members of Christ and make them members of a harlot? May it never be! Or do you not know that the one who joins himself to a harlot is one body [with her?] For He says, "THE TWO WILL BECOME ONE FLESH." But the one who joins himself to the Lord is one spirit [with Him.] Flee immorality. Every [other] sin that a man commits is outside the body, but the immoral man sins against his own body. Or do you not know that your body is a temple of the Holy Spirit who is in you, whom you have from God, and that you are not your own? For you have been bought with a price: therefore glorify God in your body. (1 Corinthians 6:15–20)

Illicit sex was not more addicting then, nor is it any less a sin now. The same Lord, who appealed through Paul to leave off that kind of immorality and join in relationships of fulfillment through God-honoring marriages, can save us and heal our land today. There is power in His blood to save us even from those sins.

We can and should form relationships of fulfillment with members of the same sex. It is God's purpose and a means of great blessing for us. One prominent example of such a relationship was the relationship between David and Jonathan in the Old Testament. We read in 1 Samuel 20:17, "Jonathan made David vow again because of his love for him, because he loved him as he loved his own life." Later, at the death of Jonathan, David cried, "I am distressed for you, my brother Jonathan; you have been very pleasant to me. Your love to me was more wonderful than the love of women" (2 Samuel 1:26).

To see the relationship between Jonathan and David as anything but holiness and godliness is to torture the context, to deny God's revelation, and to make God a liar. What we see here is confirmation that relationships of fulfillment can be achieved between members of the same sex. Among Christians who enjoy the same indwelling Holy Spirit, it should be easier and even more fulfilling.

Relationships of Fulfillment between Members of the Opposite Sex Who Are Not Married to Each Other

Can members of the opposite sex who are not married to each other form relationships of fulfillment? I believe the answer is yes, when we understand that biblical love can bring fulfillment to any relationship. Since biblical love can only be expressed in a manner consistent with God's will, it will not involve behavior that is sinful in God's eyes or that harms other individuals or the relationships of others. Entered into wisely and with the purpose of glorifying Christ, safeguards will be erected to prevent the relationship from being dashed upon the rocks of sinful passion or destroying other God-ordained relationships.

A Christian man and woman who are not married to each other are still members of the same family. They are brother and sister in Christ. There are several passages that teach how to treat members of the opposite sex outside of marriage. Paul wrote:

Do not sharply rebuke an older man, but [rather] appeal to [him] as a father, [to] the younger men as brothers, the older women as mothers, [and] the younger women as sisters, in all purity. (1 Timothy 5:1–2)

Not every Christian should automatically assume they can build relationships of fulfillment with members of the opposite sex to whom they are not married. Those who recognize in themselves a lack of self-control should avoid such relationships. Remember that the overall nature of relationships of purpose is that they first serve God and then serve the other person in the relationship. Nothing should ever be done that is not so motivated.

If either of the individuals in the relationship is married, the spouse should be a part of the relationship. He or she should know that his or her interests are being protected and served. It is imperative that limits be set on self-disclosure otherwise great harm will come to many other relationships.

The church should also be involved, so that other brothers and sisters in Christ can help to form a barrier to sin. I have known individuals who, under the guise of serving a member of the opposite sex, have violated the other person and have done great harm not only to the other person but to themselves and others. If there is even the slightest hint that the relationship is going that direction, it is better to end it immediately, for the sake of everyone involved. Fulfillment should be sought in another relationship where such dangers do not exist.

While the world apart from Christ may think they are achieving relationships of fulfillment and parade around extolling them, history tells a different story. Only those who are born again and who express genuine biblical love are able to achieve relationships of fulfillment. This kind of relationship is the crowning achievement of God's grace and love provided through His Son, Jesus Christ. Learning to building relationships God's way will overcome the ravages of the false philosophies of Gnosticism, Existentialism, and Behaviorism and enable us to reach the level of fulfillment in our relationships.

Biblical Love Produces Unity

We hear a lot about unity inside and outside the church today. The drumbeat of liberalism several decades ago has now become the drumbeat of evangelicals today. If you listen close, it has the same tempo and the same hollowness that comes from the same false philosophies: Gnosticism, Existentialism, and Behaviorism. The call is to unity, but the message is that there is no absolute truth, so any truth will do. The world is absurd; we are individually at fault, so we must create a new existence. We can accomplish all of that by changing the environment in our churches through contemporary music, creative expression, and new forms of worship. Then the world will see in us the unity that pleases men.

Not everyone who calls for unity among Christians is motivated by false philosophies. Paul commanded individual Christians to "preserve the unity of the Spirit in the bond of peace" (Ephesians 4:2). However, any unity achieved at the sake of truth is motivated by false philosophies. Jesus said, "Sanctify them in the truth, Thy word is truth." (John 17:17)

The text used by the liberals in the past is the same text to justify the new call for unity: the prayer of Jesus in John 17:20–23. Yet when we keep our Lord's prayer in context, we see that His prayer for unity flows out of the relationship He desired to have with His church once His work on the cross was complete, He ascended back to the Father, and the Holy Spirit indwelled the church. To see this in the context, we need to go back to the end of John chapter 16. Jesus said:

> These things I have spoken to you in figurative language; an hour is coming when I will speak no more to you in figurative language, but will tell you plainly of the Father. In that day you will ask in My name, and I do not say to you that I will request the Father on your behalf; for the Father Himself loves [*phileo*] you, because you have loved [*phileo*] Me and have believed that I came forth from the Father. (John 16:25–27)

As John introduced the high-priestly prayer of Jesus, he recalled how Jesus concluded His last few lessons to the disciples. In this one short statement, Jesus summarized what His relationship with His disciples would be like after His ascension and after the Holy Spirit indwells the church. It will be the ultimate expression of biblical love because it will be a relationship in which God the Father singles out as objects of His affection those who have affection for Jesus. This affection will be based on the obedient hearts made possible through rebirth and the power of the indwelling Holy Spirit. It will be a relationship of fulfillment because it will involve complete and open self-disclosure by the self-revealing God to His newly transformed creatures.

This is the unity for which Jesus prayed in John chapter 17. It is a unity of obedience, affection, and intimacy. It is the level of relationship that the three persons of the Godhead enjoy with each other. It is the level of relationship that God shares with us, and that we can enjoy with each other here on earth when we learn to love biblically. We will never achieve that kind of relationship by patterning our thinking and our lives after the world. Relationships of fulfillment can only be experienced when we first become one with God through Jesus Christ. John warned against seeking fulfillment elsewhere:

> Do not love the world, nor the things in the world. If anyone loves the world, the love of the Father is not in him. For all that is in the world, the lust of the flesh and the lust of the eyes and the boastful pride of life, is not from the Father, but is from the world. And the world is passing away, and [also] its lusts; but the one who does the will of God abides forever. (1 John 2:15–17)

Biblical Love Is the Alternative to Playing Philosophical Games

A disturbing correlation between all of the school shootings is that, as the shooters were engaged in their heinous acts, they all seemed to be acting out a game. They appeared to be characters in a drama reminiscent of a movie, video game, or some other form of entertainment.

I have chosen to describe the three philosophies of Gnosticism, Existentialism, and Behaviorism in terms of games people play. This is not to be derogatory or dismissive of those philosophies but to demonstrate the correlation between the actions of the youth involved and the philosophies so glibly believed and passed on as truth. It is one thing to sit in an ivory tower debating philosophical nuances; it is another thing to see the consequences of those false philosophies lived out in bold relief.

It is not surprising that those who promote philosophies that relieve mankind of its responsibility also refuse to accept responsibility for the havoc their philosophies inflict upon the human race. Once we understand the philosophies and their effects upon human behavior and accept the better way presented in the Bible through biblical love, we as a society will be ready to stop playing such deadly games. Then, through the power God provides, we will be ready to shoulder our God-given responsibilities, to establish healthy relationships, and to take those relationships to the level of fulfillment.

However, we must first stop playing philosophical games.

Introduction

1. *U.S. News & World Report*, May 3, 1999.
2. "Thursday's Scorecard" *The Spokesman-Review*, Thursday, April 29, 1999, A2.

Chapter One

1. W. E. Vine, Merrill F. Unger, William White, Jr., eds., *Vine's Expository Dictionary of Biblical Words*, (New York: Thomas Nelson, 1985), 66.
2. The Greek word *peripateo*.
3. The Greek word *stoicheo*.

Chapter Two

1. Jerry Leffel, Contributor, *The Death of Truth*, ed., Dennis McCallum, (Minneapolis: Bethany House Publishers, 1996), 48.
2. Ibid., 48–49.
3. William Backus and Marie Chapian, *Telling Yourself the Truth*, (Minneapolis: Bethany House Publishers, 1980).
4. Leon Festinger, *A Theory of Cognitive Dissonance*, (Stanford: Stanford University Press, 1957), 3.

5. *The New Encycolpædia Britannica* (Encyclopædia Britannica, Inc., 1997), 434.
6. Leon Festinger, Henry W. Riechen, and Stanley Schachter, *When Prophecy Fails: A Social and Psychological Study of a Modern Group That Predicted the Destruction of the World*, (New York: Harper Torchbooks, 1956), 3.

Chapter Three

1. Jerry Leffel, Contributor, *The Death of Truth*, ed., Dennis McCallum, (Minneapolis: Bethany House Publishers, 1996), 48.
2. Alexander M. Renwick, *Baker's Dictionary of Theology*, ed. Everett F. Harrison; Geoffrey W. Bromiley and Carl F. H. Henry (Grand Rapids: Baker Book House, 1966), 237.
3. Cited by Bruce Vawter, "The Fuller Sense: Some Considerations," *Catholic Biblical Quarterly*, XXVI, No. 1 (Jan., 1964), 87. Quoted by Paul Lee Tan, *The Interpretation of Prophecy*, (Winona Lake: BMH Books, 1974), 37.
4. Tan quoting Baxter, *Strategic Grasp of the Bible* (Grand Rapids, Mich.: Zondervan Pub. House, 1968), 37.
5. Kenneth Scott Latourette, *A History of Christianity*, (New York: Harper & Row, Publishers, 1953), 149.
6. Jim Leffel, Contributor, *The Death of Truth,* ed, Dennis McCallum, (Minneapolis: Bethany House Publishers, 1996), 21.
7. Ibid.
8. W. E. Vine, Merrill F. Unger, William White, Jr., eds., *Vine's Expository Dictionary of Biblical Words*, (New York: Thomas Nelson, 1985), 346–347.
9. Aorist active indicative. Cf. H. E. Dana and Julius R. Mantey, *A Manual Grammar of the Greek New Testament* (New York: Macmillan Publishing Co., Inc., 1955), 194.
10. Note Daniel B. Wallace's comment regarding the difference between the Aorist active participle and the present active participle, *Greek Grammar Beyond the Basic*, (Grand Rapids: Zondervan Publishing House, 1996), 621, fn.
11. Perfect active participle.

Chapter Four

1. *Webster's New World Dictionary of the American Language*, ed., David B. Guralnik (New York: Simon and Schuster, 1980), 491.
2. *The American Heritage Dictionary of the English Language*, Third Edition is licensed from Houghton Mifflin Company. Copyright © 1992 by Houghton Mifflin Company. All rights reserved.
3. "Existentialism," *Microsoft® Encarta® 97 Encyclopedia.* © 1993–1996 Microsoft Corporation. All rights reserved.
4. *The Concise Columbia Encyclopedia* is licensed from Columbia University Press. Copyright © 1991 by Columbia University Press. All rights reserved.
5. "Existentialism," *Microsoft® Encarta® 97 Encyclopedia.* © 1993–1996 Microsoft Corporation. All rights reserved.
6. Ibid.
7. Aorist passive participle.
8. Gene A. Getz, *Building Up One Another,* (Wheaton: Victor Books).
9. Cf. the Book of Ephesians.

Chapter Five

1. "Behaviorism," Microsoft® Encarta® 97.
2. Lawrence O. Richards, *Expository Dictionary of Bible Words,* (Grand Rapids: Regency Reference Library, 1985), 576.
3. *National Electrical Course for Apprentice: Inside Wiremen First Year Course/Student Workbook,* © 1995 by the National Joint Apprentice & Training Committee for the Electrical Industry, 27.
4. Ibid., 32.
5. Ibid.
6. Ibid.
7. Jim Leffel, "Our New Challenge: Postmodernism," *The Death of Truth,* ed. Dennis McCallum, (Minneapolis: Bethany House Publishers, 1996), 33.

Chapter Six

1. C. S. Lewis, *The Four Loves,* (New York: A Harvest/HBJ Book, 1960), 56–57.

2. Leon Morris, *Testaments of Love*, (Grand Rapids: William B. Eerdmans Publishing Company, 1981), pp. 114–115.

3. *Epithumia* is used approximately thirty-eight times and *epithueo* is used eighteen times in the Greek New Testament.

4. Ed Wheat, "Love-Life for Every Married Couple," taped message.

5. W. F. Moulton and A. S. Geden, *A Concordance to the Greek Testament*, (Edinburgh: T. & T. Clark, 1967), 367.

6. W. E. Vine, *An Expository Dictionary of New Testament Words*, (Old Tappan, N. J.: Fleming H. Revel Co., 1966), 252.

7. Hermann Cremer, *Biblico-Theological Lexicon of New Testament Greek*, (Edinburgh: T. & T. Clark, 1962), 287.

8. Friedrich Buchsel, *Theological Dictionary of the New Testament*, 9 vols. Ed. Gerhard Kittel, trans. And ed. Geoffrey W. Bromiley (Grand Rapids: Wm. B. Eerdmans Publishing Co., 1965), 3:167.

9. Ibid., 169.

10. Ibid., 171.

11. Leon Morris, *The First and Second Epistles to the Thessalonians*, (Grand Rapids: Wm B. Eerdmans Publishing Co., 1968), 124–126.

12. William F. Arndt and F. Wilbur Gengrich, *A Greek-English Lexicon of the New Testament*, (Chicago: The University of Chicago Press, 1957), 311.

13. Ethelbert Stauffer, *Theological Dictionary of the New Testament*, 9 vols. Ed. Gerhard Kittel trans. And ed. Geoffry W. Bromiley (Grand Rapids: Wm. B. Eerdmans Publishing Co., 1965), 1:37.

14. Anders Nyugren, *Agape and Eros*, (New York: Harper & Row Publishers, 1953), 173.

15. Ibid., 31.

16. *Webster's New World Dictionary of the American Language*, ed. David B. Guralnik, (New York: Simon and Schuster, 1980), s. v. "Eros," 475.

17. Ibid.

18. Richard Chenevix Trench, *Synonyms of the New Testament*, (Grand Rapids: William B. Eerdmans Publishing Co., 1966), 44.

19. Arthur D. Colman, M.D., *Love and Ecstasy*, (New York: The Seabury Press, 1975), 1.

20. A. H. Maslow, *The Meaning of Love*, ed. Ashley Montagu (New York: The Julian Press, Inc., 1953), 60.
21. James W. Davies, "An Investigation of the History of Agape and Eros from the Perspective of the Psychoanalytic Phenomenon of Transference," *Encounter*, vol. 28 (1967), 155.
22. Wheat, *Love-Life for Every Married Couple*.

Chapter Seven

1. Hermann Cremer, *Biblico-Theological Lexicon of New Testament Greek*, (Edenburgh: T. & T. Clark, 1962), 14.
2. Richard Chenevix Trench, *Synonyms of the New Testament*, (Grand Rapids: William B. Eerdmans Publishing Co., 1966), 43.
3. Leon Morris, *Love, Christian Style*, (Portland: Western Conservative Baptist Seminary, 1976), 11.
4. Kenneth S. Wuest, "Golden Nubbets," *Wuest's Word Studies from the Greek New Testament*, (Grand Rapids: Wm. B. Eerdmans Publishing Company, 1966), 60.
5. Albert Barnes, *Barnes Notes*, Electronic Database. Copyright © 1997 by Biblesoft. All rights reserved.
6. Hermann Cremer, *Biblico-Theological Lexicon of New Testament Greek*, (Edenburgh: T. & T. Clark, 1962), 12.
7. Masumi Toyotome, *Three Kinds of Love*, (Madison: InterVarsity Press, 1961), 8.
8. Anders Nyugren, *Agape and Eros*, (New York: Harper & Row Publishers, 1953), 75–81.
9. Archibald Thomas Robertson, *Word Pictures in the New Testament*, (Nashville: Broadman Press, 1932), vol. 5, 182.
10. Carl F. H. Henry, *Christian Personal Ethics*, (Grand Rapids: Wm. B. Eerdmans Publishing Co., 1957), 170.

To order additional copies of

...ABOUT MATTERS OF THIS LIFE

have your credit card ready and call

(800) 917-BOOK

or send $17.95 plus $3.95 shipping and handling to

Books, Etc.
PO Box 4888
Seattle, WA 98104

WA residents please add 8.6% sales tax ($1.54)